CLEVER QUARTERS

CLEVER QUARTERS

QUILTS FROM FAT-QUARTER CUTS

Susan Teegarden Dissmore

Martingale®
& COMPANY

Clever Quarters: Quilts from Fat-Quarter Cuts
© 2004 by Susan Teegarden Dissmore

Martingale®
& C O M P A N Y

That
Patchwork
Place®

That Patchwork Place is an imprint
of Martingale & Company®

Martingale & Company
20205 144th Avenue NE
Woodinville, WA 98072-8478
www.martingale-pub.com

Printed in China

09 08 07 06 05 04   8 7 6 5 4 3 2 1

Library of Congress Cataloging-in-Publication Data

Dissmore, Susan Teegarden
   Clever quarters / Susan Teegarden Dissmore
         p. cm.
      ISBN 1-56477-511-9
   1. Patchwork—Patterns. 2. Strip quilting—Patterns.
I. Title.
      TT835.D578 2004
      746.46'041—dc22
                        2003021715

CREDITS

President — Nancy J. Martin
CEO — Daniel J. Martin
Publisher — Jane Hamada
Editorial Director — Mary V. Green
Managing Editor — Tina Cook
Technical Editor — Ellen Pahl
Copy Editor — Erana Bumbardatore
Design Director — Stan Green
Illustrator — Robin Strobel
Cover and Text Designer — Shelly Garrison
Photographer — Brent Kane

MISSION STATEMENT
Dedicated to providing quality products
and service to inspire creativity.

The first quilt I ever owned! Lovingly made from my donated clothing scraps by Trixie Bennett, Wapato, Washington, 1976.

DEDICATION

This book is dedicated to Trixie Bennett, my "adopted" Grandma. About one year before my high school graduation, I gave Trixie a bag of scraps from clothing I had made. Unbeknownst to me, she cut those scraps into squares and sewed them into a quilt—my high school graduation gift. What a gift! It was the first quilt I ever owned, and although she has long since passed away, I do believe that somewhere, somehow, she transferred her love of quilting to me.

ACKNOWLEDGMENTS

Many of the quilts in this book were too large for me to quilt on my sewing machine. Both Eileen Peacher and Sue Gantt continue to work wonders with thread and long-arm quilting machines. They were willing to adjust their busy schedules to accommodate my book projects. I appreciate their efforts more than words can express.

Thanks to Lorri Gellerson and Stephanie Swensson, who kindly volunteered to make two last-minute projects for the book. It's great to have friends who will help at a moment's notice, especially when my tank is running on "E."

Thanks to Moda Fabrics and RJR Fashion Fabrics (wholesale fabric suppliers) who offer a wide variety of fat quarter bundles from their fabric collections. I love them! They continue to inspire the creation of quilts.

Thanks to Ellen Pahl, my editor for the third time. She has done such a great job and her efforts are much appreciated. By the end of writing a book, my brain is numb and nonfunctional. She has seen things that I totally overlooked and added that perfect word or phrase to make my sentences truly speak to you.

Thanks again to Martingale & Company for taking a chance with my book projects. I have made great strides with their continued support of my work.

Last, but never least, I need to thank my husband and sons, who look on in awe as I continue to create while they vacuum the house and fend for themselves in the kitchen!

CONTENTS

INTRODUCTION

Have you ever been at the end of a quilt project and needed just two more inches of fabric to finish that last block or border? All of the fabrics in the quilt coordinate so beautifully that a substitution is incomprehensible. You've had that well-seasoned fabric for three years, so your chances of finding it again are slim to none. But you search anyway, to no avail. If this sounds familiar, then I challenge you to experiment with my clever fat-quarter quilts. You will be rewarded with a newfound ability to add just one more fat quarter when that prized three-year-old piece runs out.

Scrap quilts are my passion! My eyes never tire of looking at them. Creating a scrap quilt requires the added effort of coordinating color in a manner that will be pleasing to all who gaze upon it. That challenge keeps me focused and excited throughout the project. It is like a jigsaw puzzle: You put all the pieces together where they fit and are delighted when the picture is finally complete.

My "scrap" quilts typically start from a coordinated collection of fat quarters that I have either created myself or purchased as a collection. If you are not ready to create your own collection, many fabric manufacturers offer fat-quarter bundles of entire collections to quilt shops. One of these early collections prompted me to create my first fat-quarter quilt, "Summer Cottage Nine Patch," on page 79. Since then, I have discovered that there is nothing more enjoyable than unbundling a tall stack of fat quarters, arranging them in color groups, and designing an entire quilt top without adding any larger cuts.

Although I didn't start designing fat-quarter quilts with a book in mind, this collection of patterns has been a work in progress for several years. As I designed the quilts, my goal was to create both small and large quilt tops that used fat quarters exclusively—no larger cuts allowed. Only two quilts, "Secrets in the Garden Runner" on page 59 and "Summer at Aunt Jane's" on page 74, have larger cuts added for borders.

This book project is so very near and dear to my heart that it gives my soul great joy to share my favorite fat-quarter quilt designs with you. I hope that you enjoy these projects as much as I have and will free yourself from that familiar trap of being "just two inches short."

Susan Teegarden Dissmore

Let's Talk about Fat Quarters

I honestly didn't know what a fat quarter was until several months after I opened my fabric shop. As customers came in search of them, I could only offer a blank stare. One day I humbly asked a customer, "Just what is a fat quarter?" Her reply was, "A fat quarter is a half-yard that is cut in half on the fold." How easy is that? I must admit, it has only been within the last few years that my appreciation for this clever little quarter-yard cut has grown!

Although it's hard to visualize a quilt shop without them, I suppose it is possible. If your favorite quilt shop does not cut or carry them, buy half-yard pieces and make your own. Just think, by making your own, you'll have two!

Clever Tip

To convert a half-yard into two fat quarters, simply fold the fabric in half, matching the selvage edges. Make a crease, open the fabric up, and cut along the fold using scissors or a rotary cutter. You now have two pieces of fabric that measure approximately 18" x 21". If you only use one half, you will have the other half to add to your fabric collection.

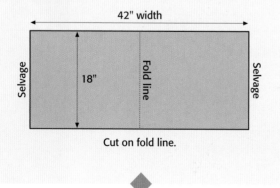

Cut on fold line.

Not all fat quarters are created equal. The standard width of quiltmaking fabric from selvage to selvage is 42". When a half-yard piece is cut in half along the fold, the resulting two pieces should be 18" x 21" each. This measurement will vary when the yardage width is more or less than the standard 42" and the half-yard itself is cut more or less than 18". Always check the measurements of your fat quarters before you start. Should you come up short, remember that you can always add a fat quarter to your project. If you happen to have more than 18" x 21", consider it your lucky day and breathe easy.

I prewash every piece of fabric before I use it in a quilt project. Prewashing adds another alteration to the final dimension of your fat quarter. You could conceivably lose up to an inch all the way around, changing the dimension to 17" x 20". Once you straighten that fat quarter, the width will shrink a little more. The projects in this book assume that the final width of your fat quarter is 17" and the length is 20" (although 21" is used in cutting lists).

Clever Fat-Quarter Tidbits

Did you know that one fat quarter can yield any one of the following?

11 strips, 1½" x 21" (great for Log Cabin blocks)

7 strips, 2½" x 21", or 56 squares, 2½" x 2½"

5 strips, 3½" x 21", or 25 squares, 3½" x 3½"

3 strips, 4½" x 21", or 12 squares, 4½" x 4½"

3 strips, 5½" x 21", or   9 squares, 5½" x 5½"

2 strips, 6½" x 21", or   6 squares, 6½" x 6½"

LET'S GET STARTED

Now that you know all about fat quarters and their dimensions, let's get started with the process of choosing them in the colors you want for your next quilt project.

Choosing Colors

I love color—all colors—but the word "color" can send even the experienced quilter running scared. If this word scares you as well, spend some extra time reading through this section. Lacking a background in art and color theory, I consider myself lucky to possess a natural gift for choosing colors for my quilts. This section will take you through my personal process in choosing fabrics, but will not offer an in-depth discussion of color theory. If my guidelines do not offer enough assistance or you want to learn more, consider purchasing a book devoted solely to the subject of color. In addition, you may also want to purchase a color wheel or other color tool.

The next step is to choose a quilt design from the book. Spend some time reviewing the materials list to determine the color, value, and scale of prints required. The materials list will offer either a color suggestion or a "value" as the fabric choice. Use the quilt photos as your preliminary guideline.

Many of the quilts in this book were created from a coordinated collection of fat quarters, with other pieces added when necessary. Most likely, you will not find the exact fabrics that I have used in these quilts, as fabric lines are often short-lived. If you've been collecting bundles, now is the time to pull out your favorite one. If you are starting from scratch, find a coordinated bundle of fat quarters at your local quilt shop to save time. If you can't find a bundle, it's time to start collecting individual fat quarters (or half-yards) in your favorite colors and in various prints to start building your fabric library. Be sure to include plaids and stripes.

When choosing individual fat quarters, start with your favorite color, disregarding its value or scale. Find that chosen color on a color wheel and work clockwise until you have gathered at least one fabric in each color family that looks good with your first choice. The quantity of coordinates is up to you. Once you have done that, it's time to think about the value and scale.

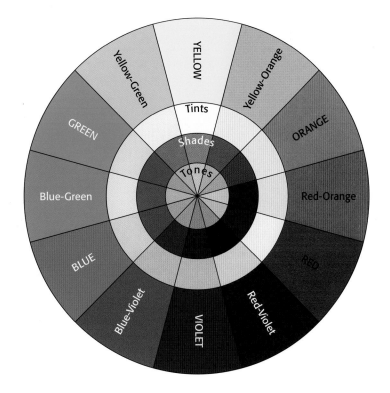

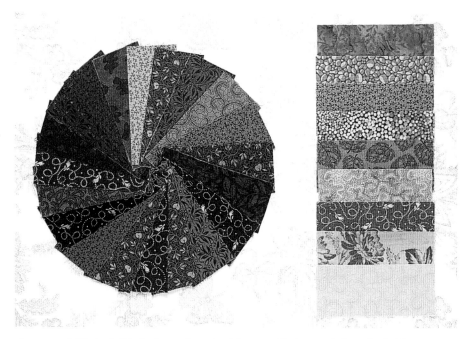

I arranged 20 dark fabrics in a color wheel format. Eighteen of those dark fabrics were used in the quilt "Connected Friends" on page 28. Although I primarily used yellow and gold as the medium values in the quilt, the row of fabrics to the right of the wheel includes other medium values that could coordinate with the dark fabrics. The background piece represents the light value.

Value is determined by the lightness or darkness of the fabric. A light fabric could be white, ivory, beige, or tan with (or without) any other color added to the print. A dark value is simply dark and a medium value is in between the light and dark. Values can vary depending on the fabric placed next to them. A medium may be a dark next to a light, but it may be a light next to a dark fabric.

Now let's expand on your first choices. Following the same color-wheel concept, pick coordinating fabrics that are lighter, in-between, or darker than the original ones. Stack them in order of your perception of lightness to darkness. Use a transparent value finder, if necessary, to see if your perception is correct. Another way to test value is to stand back at least 10 feet and look at your fabric stack while squinting. Squinting helps you see value.

Clever Tip

Value finders are transparent acrylic rectangles that come in red and green. They eliminate color so that you can readily see light, medium, and dark values. Having both colors of value finder is helpful, as a red value finder will not work well with red fabrics and a green value finder will not work well with green fabrics. They are readily available in quilt shops and catalogs.

"Scale" refers to the size of the print on the fabric. After testing the value of your fabrics, look at your stack to see how many of your prints vary in size. A mix of various scales in a quilt not only adds movement, but also keeps the eye interested. If your collection lacks a variety of scale, rethink your choices with the following guidelines.

For the quilts in this book, I consider a large-scale print one with images that are greater than 4" in diameter. These prints are typically used as a focal point within a block. A small-scale print will have images that are scattered over the cloth, and the size of those images will be considerably less than those found on large-scale prints. Many refer to these small prints as "calicoes." I like to include plaids and stripes in the same category, as they offer a fun alternative. You will also see that I use lots of tone-on-tone prints in my quilts. Tone-on-tone prints will read as a solid color, but they create the movement and interest that I like in a quilt. I use both small-scale and tone-on-tone prints to accent the large-scale pieces. I don't use true solids; I feel that they tend to stop the eye from moving across the quilt when combined with prints.

The fabrics shown are from the quilt "Susan's Subtle Stars" on page 68. The prints range from large-scale to small-scale, with some added tone-on-tone pieces. The values range from light to dark. Notice that the stripes also read as a light but offer a spark of textural contrast.

Combining all of the previously discussed elements will create your palette. Palettes are collections of fabrics that vary in scale and value and are colored in various tints, shades, and tones of a pure color. Consider the brightest, clearest fabric your pure color. Adding white to a pure color creates a pastel tint; adding black creates a deep, warm shade; adding gray creates a soft, subtle tone.

This soft pastel palette was used in the quilt "Secrets in the Garden" on page 54.

This bolder palette in rich, autumn shades was used in the quilt "Jacob's Stars" on page 46.

This subtle palette in soft tones was used in the quilt "Gentle Grace" on page 38.

Any color palette can be used with all the quilts in this book. If you don't like the palette I have chosen for the project, change it to reflect your own unique color style or preference. Treat these projects as a testing ground—a way to experiment with new color and print combinations. I promise that it will be fun and rewarding, and it will get easier as you practice, practice, practice.

Preparing Fat Quarters

I prewash all fabrics prior to their use. Fabrics will shrink at different rates and sometimes lose color. By prewashing, you may prevent a disaster later on. Wash your fabrics on the gentle cycle

with like colors and remove them from the dryer while they are still damp. Press them immediately to remove wrinkles. If desired, add spray sizing or starch when you press to add back the body and crispness that was lost during the washing process. The sizing or starch will make it easier to control your fabrics while cutting, sewing, and pressing seams.

Once your fat quarter is prewashed, you may have only a 17" x 20" piece of usable fabric. Although all cross-grain cuts in the projects have been listed as 21" in width, the yardage requirements have been calculated based on the usable width (20") to ensure that you will have adequate fabric to complete the project.

QUILTMAKING BASICS

Your fabric is chosen and prewashed. Now gather the necessary tools and supplies and review some quiltmaking basics.

TOOLS AND SUPPLIES

My advice to beginning quilters and students is to invest in the best-quality tools and supplies they can afford. This investment will make quilting easier and more accurate; both the process of making a quilt and the end result will be successful and rewarding.

Sewing Machine

First and foremost you will need a sewing machine that is in good working order. Keep your machine lint-free and well oiled (if necessary). Your machine need not be fancy, but it does need to be your friend. Get to know how your machine operates. The more you know about your machine, the better.

The stitch quality on your machine is also important. You want your stitch to be even on both sides of the fabric—not too tight or too loose. Tight tension may cause puckering; loose tension will cause your stitch to come apart. Have your machine serviced by a professional periodically to keep it in good working order. Once that is done, set up your machine for straight stitching. A setting of 12 to 14 stitches per inch is adequate for machine piecing your quilt top.

Rotary Cutter and Mat

A medium- to large-size rotary cutter is an essential tool for the projects in this book. In addition to the rotary cutter, you will need a self-healing mat. Your mat should measure at least 18" x 24".

Rulers

For rotary cutting, you'll need rulers. The ruler I find most useful when cutting strips from a fat quarter is 6" x 12". A ruler that measures 6" x 24" is useful for cutting strips from 42"-wide fabric, and it would work for fat quarters as well. I use square rulers when cutting squares from strips or squaring up blocks. The square ruler sizes I prefer are the 6½", 8", 9½", and 12½". If you need to purchase these and don't want to invest in all of them right away, start with the larger ones first.

Template Plastic

I use template plastic to aid in selective cutting. I have various sizes of squares that I keep just for this purpose. Specific use is discussed in "Selective Cutting" on page 18.

Other Basic Sewing Supplies

You will also need basic sewing supplies, including scissors for cutting thread, a seam ripper, straight pins, good-quality cotton thread, and basic sewing-machine needles. I use sizes 80/12 universal or 70/10 jeans/denim needles for machine piecing.

ROTARY CUTTING

Before you begin to cut strips from your fat quarters, you will need to straighten the edges of the fabric.

1. Fold your fat quarter in half from the one remaining selvage edge to the cut edge. Keeping the edges together, hold your fabric out in front of you, letting the fabric hang freely. Move the edges until the fabric hangs wrinkle-free. Carefully lay the folded fabric on your rotary-cutting mat with the folded edge toward you.

2. Line up a square ruler along the folded edge, and place a 6" x 12" (or 6" x 24") ruler to the left of the square ruler, keeping the ruler edges together. Remove the square ruler and cut away a small portion of the left side of the fabric. (If you are left handed, reverse this process.) You now have a clean, straight edge from which to cut strips.

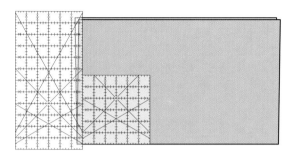

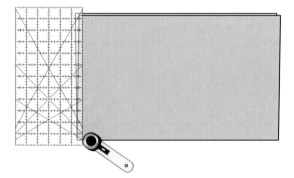

3. To cut strips, move the 6" x 12" ruler to the right, matching the ruler line for the desired width to the freshly cut edges. Cut a strip. Repeat until you have the desired number of strips.

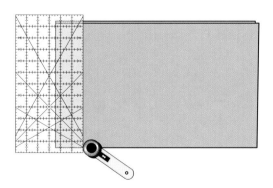

4. To cut squares from the strips, straighten one end of the strip first. Align the left side (or right side, if you're left-handed) of the strip with the desired line on the ruler. This measurement should match the strip width. Cut the desired number of squares from the strips.

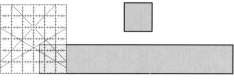

Cut squares from a strip.

5. The squares can then be left intact, cut in half diagonally once, or cut in half diagonally twice, as needed.

Square Cut Once on the Diagonal

Square Cut Twice on the Diagonal

6. To cut rectangles from strips, cut the strip width the shorter dimension of the desired rectangle. For instance, if you need rectangles that measure 2½" x 4½", cut a 2½"-wide strip, and then cut the strip into 4½"-long segments.

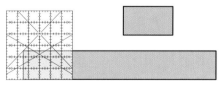

Cut rectangles from a strip.

Selective Cutting

Once in a while you may need to selectively cut a desired motif from your fat quarter. I recommend using translucent template plastic when centering a motif.

1. Cut a piece of template plastic to the finished size of the shape desired. Draw an X on the template plastic, with lines connecting opposite corners and crossing at the center.

2. Place the template plastic on your fabric and move it around until you have centered the desired motif to your satisfaction. Cut out the shape using a ruler and rotary cutter, adding ¼" on each side of the template plastic. Place your ruler carefully over the template plastic when cutting. You may want to add temporary spray adhesive or sandpaper dots to the back of the template plastic to keep it from slipping while you are cutting.

Template

◆ Clever Tip

Whenever you cut a shape from template plastic for selective cutting, write the dimensions on the sides with a permanent pen. Store the template in an envelope along with others that you make. Keep them handy for quick access when you want to do selective cutting in the future.

◆

MACHINE PIECING

Grab a comfortable chair and get an iron and ironing board ready. It's time to start piecing your quilt!

Maintaining the ¼" Seam

All of the cutting directions in this book include a ¼"-wide seam allowance. To achieve the best results in machine piecing, maintain a straight, scant ¼" seam throughout the project. Every aspect of your quilt top will be affected if you do not maintain that seam allowance.

What is a scant ¼" seam? A scant seam is one that is one or two threads smaller than an actual ¼". This allows for the space that is taken up by the thread and fabric when you press the seam to one side. To keep the seam straight, I highly recommend using a ¼" machine presser foot. If you do not have a ¼" foot available, attach an adhesive product, such as ¼" masking tape or moleskin, to the bed of your machine (not over the feed dogs). Once you have attached the foot or adhesive guide, sew two scraps together with a ¼" seam allowance and check for accuracy by holding a ruler next to the raw edge of your fabric. The thread should be just inside the ¼" line of your ruler. Adjust the position of your needle or adhesive guide until you have achieved the desired seam width.

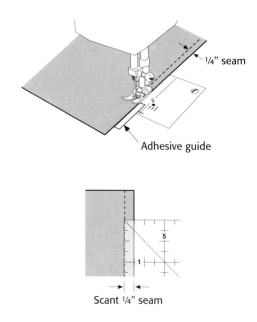

¼" seam

Adhesive guide

Scant ¼" seam

Pressing

Pressing after sewing each seam helps ensure the accuracy of your piecing. Although I have included some pressing directions with each project, the rule of thumb is to press seams to one side and usually toward the darker fabric. Occasionally, though, you may need to press a seam open to eliminate bulk. Press with a hot, dry iron set for cotton. Although I like a little steam, it can cause stretching, so be careful if you choose to apply steam to your pieces.

As you press, try to plan ahead so you will have opposing seams within your quilt blocks and the rows of your quilt top. By doing this, your seams will butt up against each other, allowing you to match seam intersections perfectly.

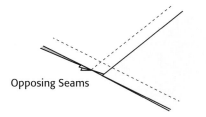

Opposing Seams

Chain Piecing

Chain piecing is a process of feeding layered pairs of triangles, patches, or strips through your sewing machine one after another. It is fast and efficient, eliminating the need to continually snip threads and thread tails. Once you have finished a chain-pieced set, feed a small piece of scrap fabric through the machine as the last piece. Snip your threads and transfer the joined pieces to your pressing surface.

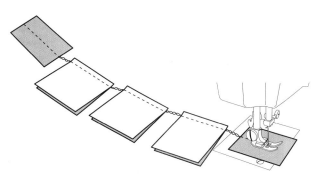

End sewing with
a thread saver.

Sewing Strip Sets

Throughout this book you will be instructed to sew strip sets. A strip set consists of two or more strips that are sewn together along their long edges. They can then be crosscut and used alone or sewn to other crosscut units to form blocks or components of blocks. Blocks that can be made from strip sets include Four Patch and Nine Patch blocks. On occasion, you may be instructed to "unsew" or remove parts of strip sets with a seam ripper to obtain a required number of units.

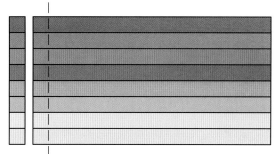

Crosscut Strip Set

Working with Triangles

Several of the blocks featured in this book use triangles. Since most of my quilts are scrappy, I usually cut triangles from squares and sew them back together individually. Extra care must be taken when sewing triangles because the center cut will be on the bias. Since bias tends to stretch, let your machine's feed dogs do all the work when sewing triangles. Triangles can be sewn into half-square- or quarter-square-triangle units, sewn to squares to create the Diamond-in-a-Square block, or used as a patch within a block.

SQUARING UP BLOCKS

When stitching components of blocks, I press and trim as I go. If a block is made up of half-square triangles, for instance, I press the seam and trim the half-square triangle to the desired unfinished size, even if it is just a few threads off as sewn. That way, it is nearly perfect when it is sewn into the finished block.

After stitching all the patches of your quilt blocks together, press and trim again, if needed. Use a large square ruler to measure the block and make sure it is the desired size plus a ¼" seam allowance on each edge. For example, if you are making 12" blocks, they should all measure 12½" before you sew them together. Be consistent with this step, making sure that all your blocks are the same size. If your blocks are not the required size, you will need to adjust all other components of the quilt accordingly.

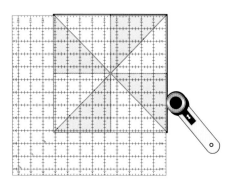

SETTING BLOCKS TOGETHER

Blocks are typically arranged in rows before being sewn together. Pin the blocks together at seam intersections to ensure that your seams line up properly. Stitch the blocks together row by row and press all the seams in one direction,

unless directed otherwise. Press seams in opposite directions from row to row for easier matching. Stitch the rows together.

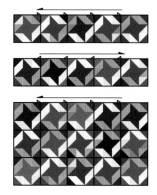

ADDING PIECED BORDERS

Most of the quilts in this book have a pieced outer border, allowing you to use your fat quarters to their fullest potential. Attaching a pieced outer border to your quilt top may require some re-pressing and seam allowance adjustments. When you are ready to attach a border unit to the quilt top, place them right sides together and pin at the seam intersections, following the guidance in the project assembly instructions. Once pinned, you can determine whether a seam needs to be re-pressed or a seam allowance adjustment is necessary.

Clever Tip

Border seams occasionally need to be re-pressed in the opposite direction of the quilt top so that seams will butt up against each other. To do this, first press the seam flat as it was when stitched. Then press to the opposite side.

If the quilt top is just slightly larger than the border strip (or vice versa), you can ease the quilt to match the length of the border strip when stitching. To do this, place the quilt top (or the border, if it is slightly longer) on the bed of your machine, with the wrong side of the border strip facing you. This allows the feed dogs to do their job; they will move the lower layer along at a slightly faster speed than the top layer. Always handle border strips carefully to avoid stretching them. Remove pins as you sew, rather than sewing over them, as they will nick and dull the machine needle.

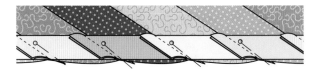

Since the intent of this book is to use fat quarters, I do not recommend adding straight-grain borders to the outer edges of the pieced borders. However, you could substitute the pieced borders with a straight-grain border if you desire. Yardage for straight-grain borders has not been included in the materials list and would need to be calculated based upon the measurement of the quilt top.

Clever Tip

If your border unit is too large, increase several seam allowances by just a thread or two. If the border unit is too small, reduce seam allowances by "unsewing" and re-sewing with a slightly smaller seam allowance until you get a good fit.

FINISHING YOUR QUILT

At this point you need to decide how you will quilt your project and whether you will need to mark the quilting designs on your quilt top. Although marking is not necessary for stitching in the ditch and some free-motion quilting, a complex design may need to be marked on the quilt top before it is layered with batting and backing.

Using 42"-wide fabric, most quilts in this book will require a pieced backing. Prewash and remove all selvage edges from your backing fabric before you sew the pieces together. The backing and batting should extend 2" to 4" beyond each edge of the finished quilt top.

Assembling the Quilt Sandwich

The next step is to make the quilt sandwich, which consists of the backing, batting, and quilt top. Your batting choice will hinge on whether you choose to machine or hand quilt. Check with your local quilt shop to choose the perfect batting for your project.

1. Lay the backing fabric, wrong side up, on a smooth, clean surface. Keep the backing fabric taut and wrinkle-free but not stretched. Secure the backing to the surface with masking tape or binder clips.

2. Lay the batting over the backing. Starting from the center, smooth out the batting until there are no wrinkles.

3. Lay the quilt top, right side up, over the batting. Starting from the center, smooth out the quilt top over the batting.

4. Pin or hand-baste the layers together. Since I machine quilt, I use #1 safety pins for basting large quilts, and basting spray for small quilts. Begin pinning in the center of the quilt and work toward the outer edges. The placement of the pins will depend on the type of machine quilting you plan to do, but place them no more than 3" apart. If you use basting spray, follow the directions with the product.

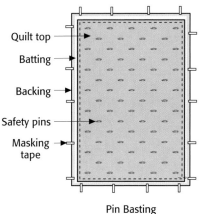

Pin Basting

5. If you plan to hand quilt, thread basting is a better choice. Sew a large grid of stitches using cotton thread. Begin in the center of the quilt and stitch about 4" to 6" apart in all directions. Make the final stitches around the outer edges of the quilt.

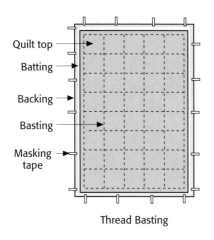

Thread Basting

6. Machine or hand quilt as desired.

Binding and Finishing

Binding is the final step in completing your quilt. I cut binding strips on the cross grain, 2½" x 42", to make a ½"-wide finished binding. For a narrower binding, cut narrower strips.

Binding

1. Cut enough strips to go around the edges of your quilt, plus an extra 12" for turning corners and joining ends. Sew the strips together with diagonal seams, forming one continuous strip Press the seams open to minimize bulk.

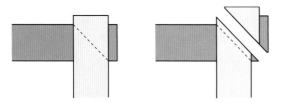

2. Press the binding strip in half lengthwise with the wrong sides together.

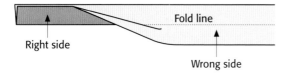

3. Position the binding all the way around the quilt, making sure that none of the seams fall at the corners of the quilt.

4. Leaving an 8" to 10" tail at the beginning, sew the binding to the quilt top with a ¼" seam allowance. Use a walking foot or dual feed mechanism to help feed all the layers through the machine evenly.

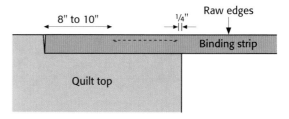

5. When you approach a corner, stop ¼" away from it. Backstitch and remove the quilt from the machine. Turn the quilt so that you will be stitching down the next side. Fold the binding up parallel to the side of the quilt, at a 45° angle. Then fold the strip down so that the fold is parallel to the top edge of the quilt and the raw edges are aligned with the side edge of the quilt. Begin sewing from the top with a ¼" seam allowance.

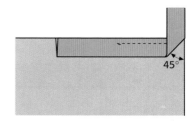

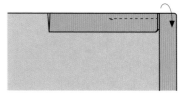

6. Continue around the quilt in this manner, stopping 8" to 10" from where you began stitching. Backstitch and remove the quilt from the machine. Trim the binding so that the beginning and ending tails overlap by 2½". (The overlap should equal the width that you cut your binding strips.)

7. Open and place the strips, right sides together, at right angles. Stitch on the diagonal and trim away the excess fabric. Press the seam open. Refold the binding and finish sewing it to the quilt.

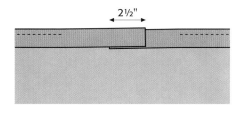

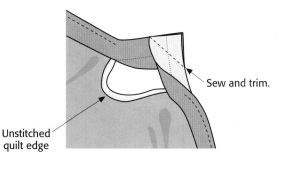

Sew and trim.

Unstitched quilt edge

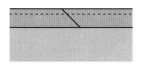

♦

Clever Tip

Press the diagonal line on the binding strip before sewing the strips together. That way, you have a guideline to follow when stitching.

♦

8. Bring the binding from the front of the quilt to the back and pin it in place if desired. It should cover the binding stitching line. Using a thread that matches the binding, whipstitch the folded edge to the back of the quilt. Be careful that your stitches do not go through to the front of the quilt. As you approach a corner, pull the binding out. With your thumbnail in the corner, fold over the unstitched binding edge, creating a miter. Secure it with stitches. Repeat for the remaining corners.

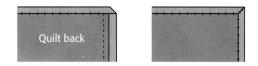

Quilt back

Adding a Label

This step only takes a few minutes and is well worth the effort. Adding a label will document information about your quilt. The label can be elaborate or plain. I like to use preprinted labels, as they are both decorative and easy to use. Using a permanent ink pen, I simply write the name of the quilt, my name, the quilter's name (if applicable), the date it was completed, and the place where it was completed. I fold under the edges of the label and whipstitch it into place. It's that simple.

A BAKER'S DOZEN

Designed, sewn, and quilted by Susan Teegarden Dissmore, 2002.

Quilt Essentials

Finished quilt: 32" x 40"

Finished block: 4" x 4"

Fat quarters: 13

This cute, nostalgic collection of fabric would sit quietly in the shop, until I walked by. Then it seemed to be calling my name, screaming for attention! The original bundle had 12 fat quarters, and I thought it would be fun to add one more to make it a "baker's dozen." What next? My mind was blank until I looked up and saw one of my clever panel quilts hanging on the wall. It had Pinwheel blocks. That was just the inspiration I needed to turn these small-scale vintage prints into this delicious little wall quilt.

MATERIALS

Yardages are based on 42"-wide fabric.

- 4 fat quarters of light prints for the blocks
- 1 fat quarter of light beige for the first inner border
- 1 fat quarter *each* of dark yellow, dark green, dark blue, and dark red for the blocks and outer border
- 1 fat quarter *each* of medium yellow, medium green, medium blue, and medium red for the blocks and outer border
- 1½ yards of fabric for backing
- ⅜ yard of fabric for binding
- 40" x 48" piece of batting

CUTTING

All measurements include ¼" seam allowances.

From *each* of the 4 light prints, cut:

- 1 strip, 3¼" x 21". Cut the strip into 6 squares, 3¼" x 3¼"; cut the squares in half diagonally twice to yield 24 triangles.
- 6 squares, 3⅜" x 3⅜" (If desired, selectively cut or cut "on point," if the print is directional.)

From the medium green and medium blue, cut:

- 1 strip, 3¼" x 21". Cut the strip into 6 squares, 3¼" x 3¼"; cut the squares in half diagonally twice to yield 24 triangles.

- 3 strips, 2⅞" x 21". Cut the strips into 16 squares, 2⅞" x 2⅞"; cut the squares in half diagonally once to yield 32 triangles (1 extra from each color).
- 2 strips, 2½" x 21"

From the dark green and dark blue, cut:

- 3 strips, 2⅞" x 21". Cut the strips into 17 squares, 2⅞" x 2⅞"; cut the squares in half diagonally once to yield 34 triangles.
- 2 strips, 2½" x 21"

From the medium yellow and medium red, cut:

- 1 strip, 3¼" x 21". Cut the strip into 6 squares, 3¼" x 3¼"; cut the squares in half diagonally twice to yield 24 triangles.
- 3 strips, 2⅞" x 21". Cut the strips into 13 squares, 2⅞" x 2⅞"; cut the squares in half diagonally once to yield 26 triangles (1 extra from each color)
- 2 strips, 2½" x 21"

From the dark yellow and dark red, cut:

- 3 strips, 2⅞" x 21". Cut the strips into 14 squares, 2⅞" x 2⅞"; cut the squares in half diagonally once to yield 28 triangles (1 extra from each color)
- 2 strips, 2½" x 21"

From the light beige, cut:

- 4 strips, 2⅞" x 21". Cut the strips into 21 squares, 2⅞" x 2⅞", and 2 squares, 2½" x 2½"; cut the 2⅞" squares in half diagonally once to yield 42 triangles.
- 2 strips, 2½" x 21". Cut the strips into 16 squares, 2½" x 2½".

ASSEMBLY

1. Using the triangles cut from the 3¼" squares, sew a light print triangle to a medium blue triangle along their short edges. Press toward the medium blue triangle. Sew a dark blue triangle cut from the 2⅞" squares to the longest edge. Press toward the dark blue triangle and trim to 2½" x 2½". Make 24 of these units.

Make 24.

2. Sew four of the units from step 1 together to form a Pinwheel block, as shown. Press the first seam toward the dark blue triangle and press the final seam open. The block should measure 4½" x 4½". Repeat to make six blocks, then make six blocks using the yellow, green, and red fabrics.

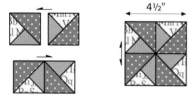

Sew 4 units together to make a Pinwheel block.

Make 6.   Make 6.

Make 6.   Make 6.

3. Using the triangles cut from the 2⅞" squares, sew a medium green triangle to one side of a 3⅜" light print square. Sew a medium blue triangle to the opposite side. Press toward the triangles. Repeat on the remaining two sides. Press and trim to 4½" x 4½". Repeat with the other colors, as shown.

Sew triangles to the sides of the light print squares.

Make 6.   Make 6.   Make 5.

Make 5.   Make 1.   Make 1.

4. Arrange and sew the blocks from steps 2 and 3 together in rows, referring to the quilt diagram for placement. Press the seam allowances of adjacent rows in opposite directions and sew the rows together to form the quilt top.

5. Using the remaining triangles cut from the 2⅞" squares, sew the medium and dark triangles to the light beige triangles along their

longest edges to form half-square-triangle units. Press toward the darker triangle and trim to 2½" x 2½".

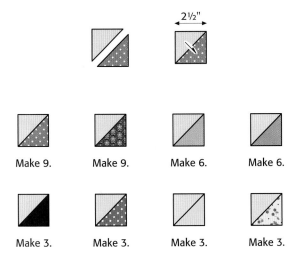

Make 9. Make 9. Make 6. Make 6.

Make 3. Make 3. Make 3. Make 3.

6. Sew the half-square-triangle units from step 5 to the 2½" light beige squares to form the first inner-border units, as shown. Press the seams in the opposite direction of the quilt edge the border will correspond to. Sew the border units to the quilt top and press as desired.

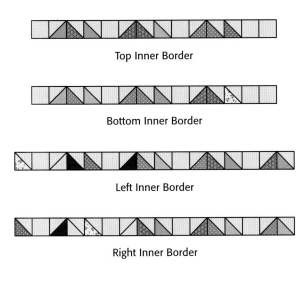

Top Inner Border

Bottom Inner Border

Left Inner Border

Right Inner Border

7. Using one of each of the colors, sew the 2½"-wide strips into two strip sets. Press in one direction. Crosscut the strip sets into a total of nine segments, each 2½" wide.

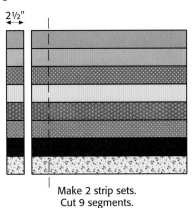

Make 2 strip sets.
Cut 9 segments.

8. Sew the crosscut segments together end to end to form one long strip. Starting at one end, count off 16 squares for the top border and "unsew" the seam. Repeat for the remaining three borders, counting 16 squares for the bottom border and 18 squares for each side border. Starting with the sides, sew the outer-border units to the quilt top, re-pressing if necessary. Press the final seam as desired.

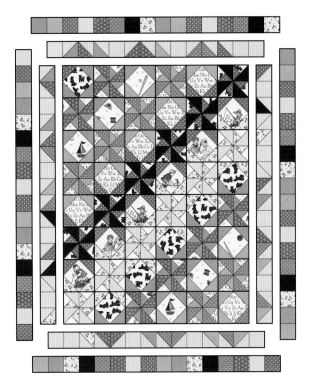

9. Quilt as desired and bind. Refer to "Finishing Your Quilt" on page 21 for more details if needed.

CONNECTED FRIENDS

Designed and sewn by Susan Teegarden Dissmore; machine quilted by Sue Gantt, 2001.

Quilt Essentials

Finished quilt: 57" x 75"
Finished block: 9" x 9"
Fat quarters: 36

I loved the colors in this collection and wanted to purchase it for the shop, but I was at the end of my fabric-buying budget. Fortunately, a fat-quarter bundle was available, allowing me to purchase the fabrics in smaller quantities. When the bundles finally arrived, I couldn't wait to start designing. From a humble Friendship Star block emerged this stunning quilt top. I combined a variety of prints in light, medium, and dark values; the value placement creates a connected link when the blocks are sewn together.

MATERIALS

Yardages are based on 42"-wide fabric.

- 18 fat quarters of assorted dark prints for the blocks and outer border
- 9 fat quarters of assorted light prints for the blocks and inner border
- 9 fat quarters of assorted medium prints for the blocks and outer border
- 3¾ yards of fabric for backing
- ⅝ yard of fabric for binding
- 65" x 83" piece of batting

CUTTING

All measurements include ¼" seam allowances.

From *each* of the 9 light prints, cut:

- 1 strip, 9½" x 21". Cut the strip to yield 2 squares, 9½" x 9½".
- 2 strips, 3½" x 21"

From *each* of the 9 medium prints, cut:

- 1 strip, 9½" x 21". Cut the strip to yield 2 squares, 9½" x 9½".
- 1 strip, 3½" x 21"

From *each* of the 18 dark prints, cut:

- 1 strip, 9½" x 21". Cut the strip to yield 2 squares, 9½" x 9½".
- 2 strips, 3½" x 21". Reserve 1 strip from each print. From each remaining strip, cut 2 squares, 3½" x 3½", for a total of 36 (1 extra square).

ASSEMBLY

The 35 blocks in this quilt require lots of half-square-triangle units. To simplify the cutting and sewing process, I used the Bias Square method developed by Nancy J. Martin.

1. Stack two different darks, one light, and one medium 9½" square, aligning the raw edges and keeping right sides up.

2. Cut the pieces in half diagonally once through the center. From the center, cut strips 3" wide. The triangular pieces on the sides must also be at least 3" wide.

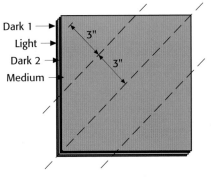

Layer 2 darks, a medium and a light, right sides facing up. Cut as indicated.

3. Arrange the strips together as shown to make four strip sets.

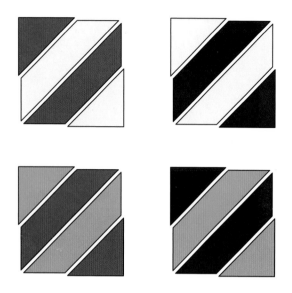

4. Sew the strips together and press the seams toward the dark fabric. The left sides of the strips should be even. The opposite end of the strips will be uneven.

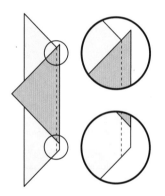

Make 1 (dark 1 and light).   Make 1 (dark 2 and light).

Make 1 (dark 1 and medium).   Make 1 (dark 2 and medium).

5. Starting in the lower left corner, align the 45° line of a square ruler with a seam line. Align the edges at approximately 3¾" to make the first cut slightly oversize. Cut two sides of the square. Then rotate the square and cut the remaining two sides to 3½". Work left to right on the strip set until all the half-square triangles have been cut. Each strip set should yield four squares, 3½" x 3½", for a total of 16 squares for each grouping of light, medium, and dark fabrics. Repeat steps 1 through 5 until all fabric groupings have been sewn together and cut into half-square-triangle units. You should be able to cut 288 half-square-triangle units, giving you eight extra.

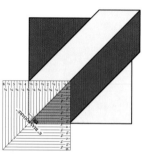

3½"

3½"

Clever Tip

When cutting squares from the strip sets, I find that a 4" or 6" square ruler works best. A larger square ruler may be cumbersome. The square ruler should have a diagonal line through the center marking the 45° angle.

6. Lay out the half-square triangles and the matching 3½" center squares, and sew them into rows. Press the top and bottom rows toward the outer unit and press the center row toward the center square. Sew the rows together to form the block. Press all the seams in one direction. Each block should measure 9½" x 9½". Make 35 blocks.

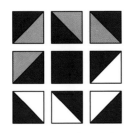

Placement of Light, Medium, and Dark Values

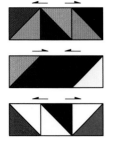 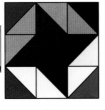

Make 35.

7. Using a design wall or other surface, arrange the blocks in rows. Rotate every other block 180° to create the connection.

8. Sew the blocks together in rows and press each row in the opposite direction. Sew the rows together to form the quilt top.

9. Using the light 3½" x 21" strips, sew two strip sets of nine strips each. Press in one direction. Crosscut the strip sets into nine segments, 3½" wide.

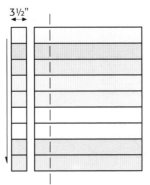

Make 2 strip sets.
Cut 9 segments.

10. Sew the segments together end to end to form one long strip for the light border.

11. Count off 17 squares for the top border and "unsew" the next seam. Count off 21 squares for the first side border, and unsew again. Then unsew the next 17 squares for the bottom border and the next 21 squares for the last side border.

12. Sew the sets of 21 squares to the sides of the quilt and press toward the border. Sew the sets of 17 squares to the top and bottom and press toward the border again.

13. Repeat step 9 using the dark and medium 3½" x 21" strips. Make three strip sets of nine strips each. Press in one direction. Cut segments from each of the strip sets for a total of 10 segments, 3½" wide. You will have extra of the strip sets, but this will give you more variety in your pieced border.

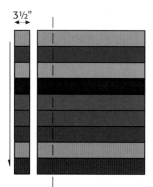

3½"

Make 3 strip sets.
Cut 10 segments.

14. Sew the segments together end to end to form one long strip. Count off 19 squares for the top border and unsew. Unsew again after counting off the next 23 squares for the first side border, the next 19 squares for the bottom border, and 23 squares for the remaining side border.

15. With seams pressed in the opposite direction of the light squares, sew the sets of 23 squares to the sides of the quilt. Press toward the outer border. Sew the sets of 19 squares to the top and bottom of the quilt. Press toward the outer border again.

16. Quilt as desired and bind. Refer to "Finishing Your Quilt" on page 21 for more details if needed.

MAGIC TABLE RUNNER

Runner on left: sewn and quilted by Sara O'Donnell, 2002.
Runner on right: designed, sewn, and quilted by Susan Teegarden Dissmore, 2001.

Quilt Essentials

Finished runner (option one): 14" x 50½"
Finished runner (option two): 14½" x 40"
Finished block: 6" x 6"
Fat quarters: 6

I once purchased an entire collection of fabric for the shop that I thought was perfect for a fat-quarter quilt I had designed. I made up the sample and proceeded to cut the entire collection into fat-quarter bundles. Not everyone agreed with my idea, so I was forced to figure a way out of the mess I had created! I unbundled one of the fat-quarter packs and found that they could be re-bundled into groups of six. Magically, at that moment a lightbulb flashed on in my head, and this easy table runner with two border options was the result. Now I have used this pattern in my shop many times. I love this table runner—it's simple, quick to make with favorite fabrics, and it solved my problem! If you have ever bought a collection of fabrics and then wondered why, you will love this project, too!

MATERIALS

Yardages are based on 42"-wide fabric.

- 3 fat quarters for the Nine Patch blocks (fabrics A, B, and C)*
- 1 fat quarter for the setting triangles (fabric D)
- 1 fat quarter for the inner border (fabric E)
- 1 fat quarter for the outer border (fabric F)
- ⅞ yard of fabric for backing for option 1
- ¾ yard of fabric for backing for option 2
- ⅜ yard of fabric for binding
- 20" x 59" piece of batting for option 1
- 20" x 48" piece of batting for option 2

Whichever fabric you designate as fabric A will be the center of the Nine Patch blocks. It will create the vertical "chain" in the center of the table runner.

Clever Tip

This table runner is perfect for showcasing some of your favorite fat quarters. Use your favorites for the setting triangles, the center of the Nine Patch blocks, and the borders.

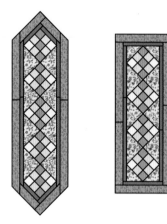

Option 1   Option 2
Border Options

CUTTING

All measurements include ¼" seam allowances.

From fabric A, cut:

- 3 strips, 2½" x 21"

From fabric B, cut:

- 4 strips, 2½" x 21"

From fabric C, cut:

- 2 strips, 2½" x 21"

From fabric D, cut:

Option 1

- 2 squares, 9¾" x 9¾". Cut each square in half diagonally twice to yield 8 triangles.

Option 2

- 2 squares, 9¾" x 9¾". Cut each square in half diagonally twice to yield 8 triangles (2 extra triangles).
- 2 squares, 5⅛" x 5⅛". Cut each square in half diagonally once to yield 4 triangles for the corners.

From fabric E, cut:

- 6 strips, 1½" x 21"

From fabric F, cut:

Option 1

- 7 strips, 2¼" x 21"

Option 2

- 6 strips, 2½" x 21"

QUILT ASSEMBLY

1. Using the strips cut from fabrics A, B, and C, sew three strip sets, as shown. Press toward fabric B.

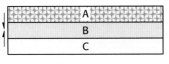

Make 2 strip sets.

Make 1 strip set.

2. Crosscut *each* of the strip sets into five segments, 2½" wide, for option 1. Cut four segments, 2½" wide, for option 2. Sew the crosscut segments together as shown to form the Nine Patch blocks. Press.

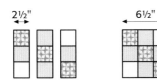

Make 5 for option 1.
Make 4 for option 2.

3. Sew the triangles cut from the 9¾" squares to the sides of each Nine Patch block, as shown. Press toward the triangles and trim the dog ears.

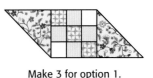

Make 3 for option 1.
Make 2 for option 2.

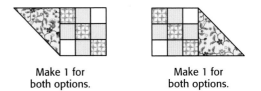

Make 1 for both options.

Make 1 for both options.

4. Sew the units from step 3 together, as shown. Press toward the triangles and trim the dog ears. For option 2, sew the triangles cut from the 5⅛" squares to the ends of the blocks, as shown.

Option 1   Option 2

BORDER ASSEMBLY FOR OPTION 1

1. Sew a 1½"-wide strip cut from fabric E to one side of the Nine Patch block at the end of the runner. Press toward the strip. Trim the tail even with the side of the runner, as shown. Repeat on the other side of the Nine Patch block.

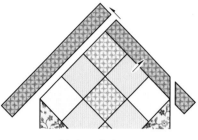

Stitch and trim even.

2. Repeat step 1 on the other end of the runner.

3. Sew two of the remaining 1½"-wide strips cut from fabric E together end to end, forming one long strip. Repeat with the last two strips. Sew these strips to each side of the runner, leaving tails on both ends. Press toward the strip and trim the ends, as shown.

4. Repeat steps 1 through 3 using the 2¼"-wide strips cut from fabric F.

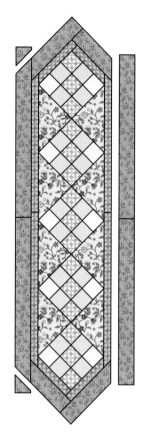

Clever Tip

If you prefer straight-grain, unpieced outer borders, replace the fabric F fat quarter and the backing fabric with 1½ yards of one piece. From that, cut three strips the desired border width parallel to the selvage edge. Use the remaining fabric for the backing of your table runner.

BORDER ASSEMBLY FOR OPTION 2

1. Sew two of the 1½" strips cut from fabric E together end to end to form one long strip. Repeat with two more strips. Measure the runner from end to end, and cut the pieced strips to that measurement. Sew these strips to each side of the runner. Press toward the strips. Measure the runner from side to side, including the inner border, and cut the remaining two strips to that length. Sew these strips to each end of the runner. Press toward the strips.

2. Repeat step 1 using the 2½"-wide strips cut from fabric F.

FINISHING

1. Cut the backing fabric lengthwise through the center. Sew the pieces together end to end to form a piece 21" x 63" for option 1 or 21" x 54" for option 2.

2. Quilt as desired and bind. Refer to "Finishing Your Quilt" on page 21 for more details if needed.

Clever Tip

If you like to appliqué, choose subtle prints for the center of the table runner; use it as a lovely pieced background for appliqué designs. Or you can purchase yardage to cut wider borders and add appliqués to the outer borders.

GENTLE GRACE

Designed and sewn by Susan Teegarden Dissmore; machine quilted by Eileen Peacher, 2003.

Quilt Essentials

Finished quilt: 63" x 81"

Finished block: 9" x 9"

Fat quarters: 55

On occasion, I purchase fabric just for me, not for the shop. I call this "fabric for the soul." This fabric collection waited patiently in my fabric closet for about two years before inspiration finally struck. As I repeatedly sorted through these lovely prints, a vertical design began to float around in my thoughts. Before the idea floated away, I began to sketch some drawings on my computer. The result is "Gentle Grace," my "quilt for the soul."

MATERIALS

Yardages are based on 42"-wide fabric.

- 12 fat quarters of light beige for the logs
- 8 fat quarters of dark green for the corner-stones
- 7 fat quarters of medium coral for the Diamond-in-a-Square blocks and the outer border
- 6 fat quarters of dark plum for the Diamond-in-a-Square blocks and the outer border
- 5 fat quarters of large-scale floral prints for the Diamond-in-a-Square block centers
- 4 fat quarters *each* of medium blue, medium green, and medium yellow for the Diamond-in-a-Square blocks and the logs
- 2 fat quarters of light green wavy prints for the Diamond-in-a-Square blocks
- 2 fat quarters of light blue wavy prints for the Diamond-in-a-Square blocks
- 1 fat quarter of a light plum wavy print for the Diamond-in-a-Square blocks
- 5 yards of fabric for backing
- ¾ yard of fabric for binding
- 71" x 89" piece of batting

CUTTING

All measurements include ¼" seam allowances.

From the dark green, cut:

- 78 strips, 1½" x 21"

From the light beige, cut:

- 10 strips, 5½" x 21"
- 3 strips, 7½" x 21"
- 3 strips, 3½" x 21"
- 54 strips, 1½" x 21"

From 1 light green wavy print, cut:

- 10 squares, 3⅜" x 3⅜"; cut the squares in half diagonally once to yield 20 triangles.

From the second light green wavy print, cut:

- 8 squares, 3⅜" x 3⅜"; cut the squares in half diagonally once to yield 16 triangles.

From *each* light blue wavy print, cut:

- 8 squares, 3⅜" x 3⅜"; cut the squares in half diagonally once to yield 16 triangles.

From the light plum wavy print, cut:

- 8 squares, 3⅜" x 3⅜"; cut the squares in half diagonally once to yield 16 triangles.

From the medium coral, cut:

- 4 strips, 7½" x 21"
- 4 strips, 5½" x 21"
- 4 strips, 3½" x 21"
- 11 strips, 1½" x 21"
- 8 squares, 4⅛" x 4⅛"; cut the squares in half diagonally once to yield 16 triangles.

From the dark plum, cut:

- 1 strip, 7½" x 21"
- 1 strip, 5½" x 21"
- 1 strip, 3½" x 21"
- 34 strips, 1½" x 21"
- 8 squares, 4⅛" x 4⅛"; cut the squares in half diagonally once to yield 16 triangles.

From the medium blue, cut:

- 15 strips, 1½" x 21"
- 8 squares, 4⅛" x 4⅛"; cut the squares in half diagonally once to yield 16 triangles.

From the medium green, cut:

- 13 strips, 1½" x 21"
- 10 squares, 4⅛" x 4⅛"; cut the squares in half diagonally once to yield 20 triangles.

From the medium yellow, cut:

- 13 strips, 1½" x 21"
- 8 squares, 4⅛" x 4⅛"; cut the squares in half diagonally once to yield 16 triangles.

From the large-scale floral prints, selectively cut:

- 21 squares, 5" x 5"

ASSEMBLY

1. Sew seven dark green 1½" x 21" strips to the top of seven light beige 5½" x 21" strips. Press toward the dark green strip. Crosscut the strip sets into 84 segments, 1½" x 6½".

Make 7 strip sets.
Cut 84 segments.

2. Sew wavy print triangles cut from the light green, light blue, and light plum 3⅜" squares to 21 of the light beige 1½" x 21" strips, leaving a 1½" gap between each triangle. (You can sew four triangles to each strip.) Press toward the triangle. Trim one side straight across and the other side at a 45° angle, as shown. Sew the triangle to the unit from step 1. Press and trim the uneven edge to a 45° angle, as shown.

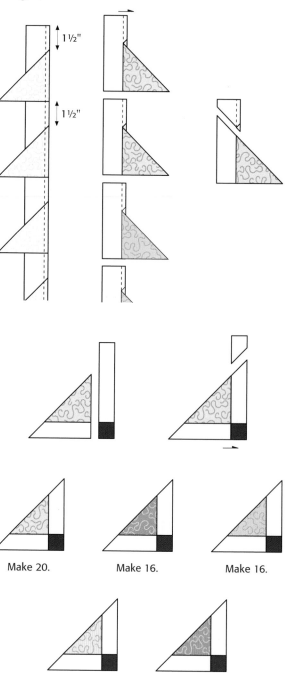

Make 20.   Make 16.   Make 16.

Make 16.   Make 16.

3. Sew the triangles cut from the medium coral, dark plum, medium blue, medium green, and medium yellow 4⅛" squares to each side of the large-scale floral squares. The triangles are cut just slightly oversize. Press toward the triangles and be sure that you trim to 6⅞" x 6⅞".

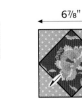

6⅞"

4. Sew the units from step 2 to each side of the square from step 3. Press toward the pieced corner triangles and trim to 9½" x 9½". Make the blocks in the color combinations and quantities shown.

9½"

Make 5.   Make 4.

Make 4.   Make 4.

Make 4.

Clever Tip

To center and sew a triangle to a square, first fold both pieces in half. Finger-press a crease on the fold. With right sides together, line up the fold lines, pin, and stitch.

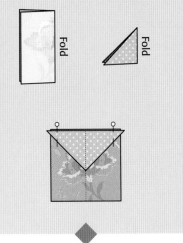

Fold   Fold

5. Sew the 1½" x 21" strips together to make strip sets in the quantities and color combinations shown. Press toward the dark green. Crosscut the strip sets into 1½" x 3½" segments, as shown.

6. Sew the crosscut segments together to form Nine Patch blocks in the color combinations shown. Press.

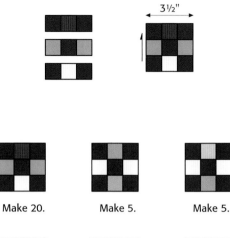

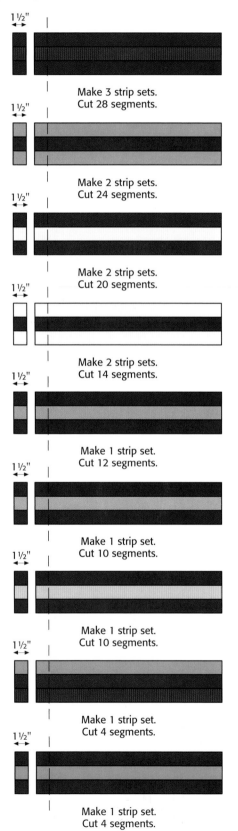

Make 3 strip sets.
Cut 28 segments.

Make 2 strip sets.
Cut 24 segments.

Make 2 strip sets.
Cut 20 segments.

Make 2 strip sets.
Cut 14 segments.

Make 1 strip set.
Cut 12 segments.

Make 1 strip set.
Cut 10 segments.

Make 1 strip set.
Cut 10 segments.

Make 1 strip set.
Cut 4 segments.

Make 1 strip set.
Cut 4 segments.

Make 20.

Make 5.

Make 5.

Make 4.

Make 4.

Make 2.

Make 1.

Make 1.

7. Sew the dark green 1½" x 21" strips to each side of the medium coral 7½" x 21" strips. Repeat with the medium coral 5½" x 21" and 3½" x 21" strips. Press toward the dark green and crosscut each group of strip sets into 52 segments, 1½" wide.

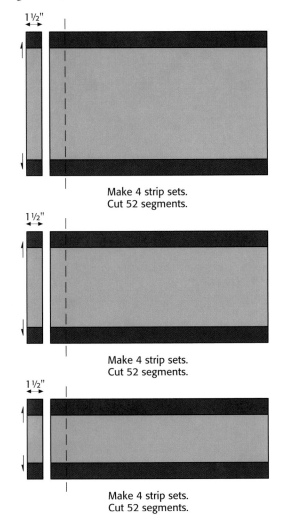

Make 4 strip sets.
Cut 52 segments.

Make 4 strip sets.
Cut 52 segments.

Make 4 strip sets.
Cut 52 segments.

8. Repeat step 7 using the dark green and light beige strips. Crosscut each group of strip sets into 28 segments, 1½" wide.

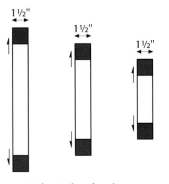

Make 3 of each strip set.
Cut 28 segments from each group.

9. Repeat step 7 using the dark green and dark plum strips. Crosscut each strip set into four segments, 1½" wide.

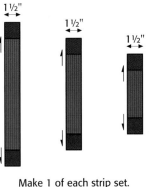

Make 1 of each strip set.
Cut 4 segments from each.

10. With right sides together, chain-piece the 20 Nine Patch blocks (of the same color combination) from step 6 to dark plum 1½" x 21" strips. Press toward the Nine Patch block and trim to 3½" x 4½".

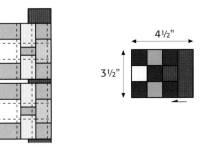

11. With right sides together, chain-piece the units from step 10 to a light beige 1½" x 21" strip. Press toward the Nine Patch block and trim to 3½" x 5½".

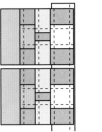
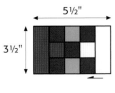

12. Sew two of the crosscut segments from step 7 to each side of the unit from step 11. Press toward the block center and trim to 5½" x 5½", if necessary.

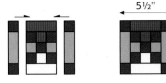

13. Continue to add strips on each side as shown, until the block is complete. Press toward the block centers and trim as you go, if needed.

Each block should measure 9½" x 9½". Repeat to sew blocks in the color combinations and quantities shown.

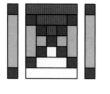 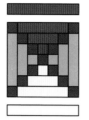 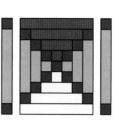 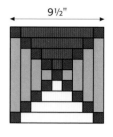

9½"

Piece all color combinations shown below, following steps 11 through 13.

  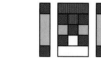 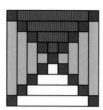 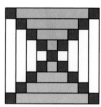

Make 20.

Make 5.

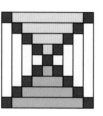 

Make 5.

Make 4.

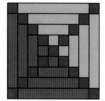

Make 4.

Make 2.

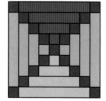 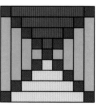

Make 1.

Make 1.

14. Sew the blocks together in vertical rows, referring to the quilt diagram for placement. Press the rows in opposite directions.

15. Sew the rows together to form the quilt top.

16. Quilt as desired and bind. Refer to "Finishing Your Quilt" on page 21 for more details if needed.

JACOB'S STARS

Designed and sewn by Susan Teegarden Dissmore; machine quilted by Eileen Peacher, 2002.

Quilt Essentials

Finished quilt: 69" x 87"
Finished blocks: 9" x 9"
Fat quarters: 46

Every time someone sees this quilt, I hear the same thing: "I just want to curl up in it!" This quilt is one of my favorites, but there is a trick to it. To select fabric, start with the 6 leaf prints. From there, choose 6 coordinating dark colors (such as blue, green, purple, rust or red, brown, and black). Once you've selected the first set of 6 dark colors, choose 4 more prints repeating some of the colors, for a total of 10 dark prints. From that point, select 10 coordinating medium-value prints and 6 plaids. Any beige prints should work with your color choices.

MATERIALS

Yardages are based on 42"-wide fabric.

- 12 fat quarters of assorted light beige prints (8 for the blocks and 4 for the outer border)
- 10 fat quarters of assorted medium prints (6 for the blocks and 4 for the outer border)
- 10 fat quarters of assorted dark prints (6 for the blocks and 4 for the outer border)
- 6 fat quarters of assorted leaf prints (6 for the Star block centers and 4 for the outer border)
- 6 fat quarters of assorted plaids for the blocks
- 2 fat quarters of black tone-on-tone prints for the outer border
- 5½ yards of fabric for backing
- ¾ yard of fabric for binding
- 78" x 96" piece of batting

CUTTING

All measurements include ¼" seam allowances.

From *each* of the 6 plaids, cut:

- 4 strips, 2" x 21"
- 1 strip, 4¼" x 21". Cut the strip into 4 squares, 4¼" x 4¼"; cut the squares in half diagonally twice to yield 16 triangles.

From *each* of 6 medium prints, cut:

- 4 strips, 2" x 21"
- 2 strips, 3⅞" x 21". Cut the strip into 8 squares, 3⅞" x 3⅞"; cut the squares in half diagonally once to yield 16 triangles.

From *each* of 4 medium prints, cut:

- 4 strips, 2⅝" x 21"
- 1 strip, 4¼" x 21". Cut the strip into 4 squares, 4¼" x 4¼"; cut the squares in half diagonally twice to yield 16 triangles.

From *each* of 6 dark prints, cut:

- 2 strips, 3⅞" x 21". Cut the strips into 8 squares, 3⅞" x 3⅞"; cut the squares in half diagonally once to yield 16 triangles.
- 2 strips, 4¼" x 21". Cut the strips into 8 squares, 4¼" x 4¼"; cut the squares in half diagonally twice to yield 32 triangles.

From _each_ of 4 dark prints, cut:

- 4 strips, 2⅝" x 21"

From _each_ of 8 light beige prints, cut:

- 3 strips, 3⅞" x 21". Cut the strips into 12 squares, 3⅞" x 3⅞"; cut the squares in half diagonally once to yield 24 triangles.

- 1 strip, 4¼" x 21". Cut the strip into 4 squares, 4¼" x 4¼"; cut the squares in half diagonally twice to yield 16 triangles (4 extra triangles).

From _each_ of 4 light beige prints, cut:

- 4 strips, 2⅝" x 21"

From _each_ of the 6 leaf prints, cut:

- 1 strip, 3½" x 21". Cut the strip into 4 squares, 3½" x 3½".

From _each_ of 4 leaf prints, cut:

- 4 strips, 2⅝" x 21"

From _each_ of the 2 black tone-on-tone prints, cut:

- 4 strips, 4¼" x 21". Cut the strips into 13 squares, 4¼" x 4¼"; cut the squares in half diagonally twice to yield 52 triangles.

ASSEMBLY

1. To make the Jacob's Ladder blocks, arrange the plaid and medium print 2" strips into pairs. You will have six sets of four pairs each. Sew the strips into 24 strip sets, four of each color combination. Press toward the medium print and crosscut the strip sets into a total of 240 segments, 2" wide.

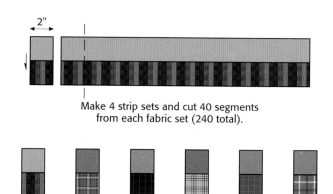

Make 4 strip sets and cut 40 segments from each fabric set (240 total).

Cut 40. Cut 40. Cut 40. Cut 40. Cut 40. Cut 40.

2. Sew the segments from step 1 together to make the four-patch units. Press. Each unit should measure 3½" x 3½". Make 120.

3½"

Make 20 from each fabric set (120 total).

Make 20. Make 20. Make 20.

Make 20. Make 20. Make 20.

48

3. Sew the dark print and light beige triangles cut from 3⅞" squares together along their longest edges to form half-square-triangle units. Press toward the dark print. Trim the blocks to 3½" x 3½". Make 96.

4. Sew the units from steps 2 and 3 together in rows. Press toward the four-patch units. Sew the rows together to form the Jacob's Ladder block. Press the seams in one direction. Each block should measure 9½" x 9½".

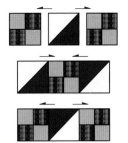

Make 16 from each fabric set (96 total).

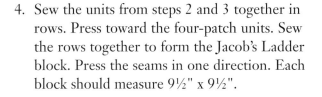

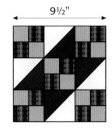

Make 4 from each fabric set (24 total).

Make 16.   Make 16.   Make 16.

Make 16.   Make 16.   Make 16.

Make 4.   Make 4.   Make 4.

Make 4.   Make 4.   Make 4.

5. To make the Star blocks, sew the triangles cut from the medium-print 3⅞" squares to the light beige triangles cut from the 3⅞" squares along their longest edges to form half-square-triangle units. Press toward the medium print. Trim the dog ears and trim the block to 3½" x 3½". Make 96.

3½"

Make 16 from each fabric set (96 total).

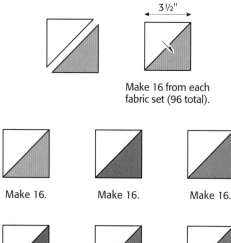

Make 16.　　Make 16.　　Make 16.

Make 16.　　Make 16.　　Make 16.

6. Using the triangles cut from the dark, plaid, and light beige 4¼" squares, sew a dark triangle to a plaid triangle along a short edge. Press toward the dark. Make 96. Repeat using a dark triangle and a light beige triangle. Make 96.

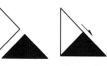

Make 16 from each fabric set (96 total).　　Make 16 from each fabric set (96 total).

7. Sew the units from step 6 together to form quarter-square-triangle units. Press. Trim the block to 3½" x 3½".

3½"

Make 16 from each fabric set (96 total).

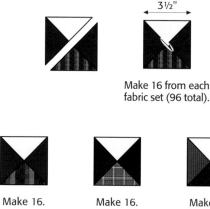

Make 16.　　Make 16.　　Make 16.

Make 16.　　Make 16.　　Make 16.

8. Sew the units from steps 5 and 7 together in rows with the 3½" leaf print squares and press the seams, as shown. Sew the rows together to form the Star block. Press. Each block should measure 9½" x 9½".

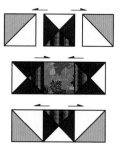
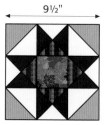
9½"

Make 4 from each fabric set (24 total).

Make 4.　　Make 4.　　Make 4.

Make 4.　　Make 4.　　Make 4.

9. Arrange and sew the Jacob's Ladder and Star blocks together in rows, as shown. Press rows in opposite directions. Re-press the blocks if necessary. Sew the rows together to form the quilt top.

Clever Tip

Using a design surface, I arranged the Jacob's Ladder blocks first. Working from left to right and from top to bottom, I laid them out by color. If you look carefully at the quilt, you will see the repeated color sequence of these blocks. Once you have arranged the Jacob's Ladder blocks, place the Star blocks around them, away from like prints.

10. Arrange the 2⅝"-wide strips into four different color sets, each consisting of a light, leaf print, medium, and dark strip. Sew the strips together into sets in a light-to-dark color sequence, as shown. Press two of the color combinations in one direction and the remaining two color combinations in the opposite direction. Crosscut the strip sets into 2⅝"-wide segments (25 each of the four color combinations).

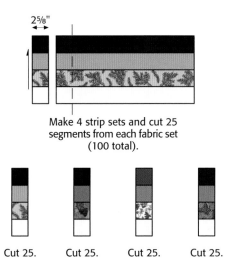

Make 4 strip sets and cut 25 segments from each fabric set (100 total).

Cut 25.   Cut 25.   Cut 25.   Cut 25.

11. Sew a black triangle to the top of each unit from step 10. Press in the same direction you did in step 10 and trim the dog ears.

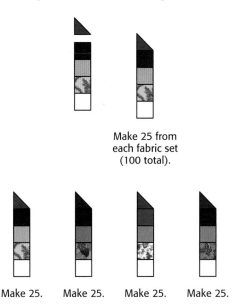

Make 25 from each fabric set (100 total).

Make 25.   Make 25.   Make 25.   Make 25.

12. Sew 56 medium and 28 light beige triangles cut from 4¼" squares to the bottoms of the units from step 11. Press and trim the dog-ears.

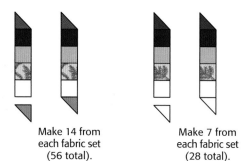

Make 14 from each fabric set (56 total).

Make 7 from each fabric set (28 total).

13. Sew the units from step 12 together to form the outer borders, sewing together 18 for the top and bottom borders and 24 for the side borders, alternating the color combinations as you sew. Press.

Top and Bottom Border
Make 2.

Side Border
Make 2.

14. Sew the remaining units from step 11 together to form the corner outer border pieces, as shown. Remove squares as you sew. Press. Sew a black triangle to one end. Press.

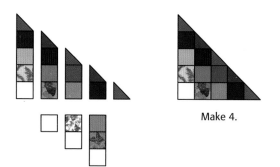

Make 4.

15. Sew the corner units from step 14 to one end of each of the border units from step 13. Press.

Clever Tip

Handle the border units with extreme care. The edges are cut on the bias and will stretch easily if pressed or pulled too hard. If your border units are too large, slightly enlarge the seam allowances between segments. Place the border units on the bed of your machine when sewing them to the quilt top. This will also help ease them in.

16. Sew the borders to the quilt one side at a time, mitering the corners as you go. Press.

17. Quilt as desired and bind. Refer to "Finishing Your Quilt" on page 21 for more details if needed.

Secrets in the Garden

Designed and sewn by Susan Teegarden Dissmore; machine quilted by Eileen Peacher, 2003.

Quilt Essentials

Finished quilt: 56" x 68"

Finished block: 12" x 12"

Fat quarters: 40

I just can't seem to resist softly colored floral prints like the ones in this quilt! They feel so old-fashioned and nostalgic, with the large cabbage roses and other flowers from cutting gardens. The quilts I make from these irresistible collections will someday become part of a lovely bedroom ensemble. Have fun choosing your own favorites for this garden-inspired quilt.

MATERIALS

Yardages are based on 42"-wide fabric.

- 10 fat quarters of assorted light beige prints
- 5 fat quarters of assorted floral prints with background colors of blue, pink, yellow, green, and lavender
- 5 fat quarters *each* of assorted blue, pink, yellow, green, and lavender prints
- 3⅝ yards of fabric for backing
- ⅝ yard of fabric for binding
- 64" x 76" piece of batting

CUTTING

All measurements include ¼" seam allowances.

From *each* of the 5 assorted blue, pink, and yellow prints, cut:

- 4 strips, 2½" x 21". Cut the strips into 8 rectangles, 2½" x 4½", and 15 squares, 2½" x 2½" (3 extra squares per color set).

From *each* of the 5 assorted green and lavender prints, cut:

- 4 strips, 2½" x 21". Cut the strips into 8 rectangles, 2½" x 4½", and 14 squares, 2½" x 2½" (2 extra rectangles per color set).

From *each* of 4 assorted blue, pink, yellow, green, and lavender prints, cut:

- 1 strip, 4⅞" x 21". Cut the strip into 3 squares, 4⅞" x 4⅞"; cut the squares in half diagonally once to yield 6 triangles.

From *each* of the 10 light beige prints, cut:

- 2 strips, 4⅞" x 21". Cut the strips into 6 squares, 4⅞" x 4⅞"; cut the squares in half diagonally once to yield 12 triangles.

From *each* of the 5 floral prints, selectively cut:

- 4 squares, 4½" x 4½"

ASSEMBLY

1. With right sides together, place a pink 2½" square on one corner of a yellow 2½" x 4½" rectangle. Draw a line through the center of each square, as shown, and stitch on the line. Trim away the excess fabric, leaving a ¼" seam. Press toward the pink triangle. Repeat on the other side of the rectangle. Press.

2. Repeat step 1, making flying-geese units in the color combinations and quantities listed. Trim to 2½" x 4½" if necessary.

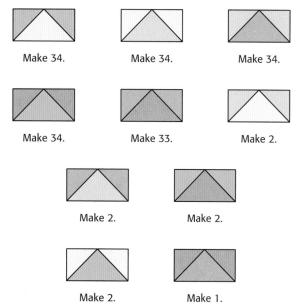

Make 34.   Make 34.   Make 34.

Make 34.   Make 33.   Make 2.

Make 2.   Make 2.

Make 2.   Make 1.

3. With right sides together, sew a light beige triangle to a pink triangle along the longest edge to form a half-square-triangle unit. Press toward the pink triangle and trim to 4½" x 4½". Repeat for each color combination shown.

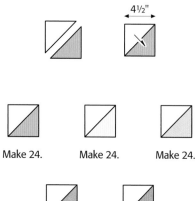

4½"

Make 24.   Make 24.   Make 24.

Make 24.   Make 24.

4. Sew two like flying-geese units together to form a 4½" x 4½" square. Add the 4½" floral center squares and the half-square-triangle units from step 3 to form the blocks. Sew the units together in rows. Press as shown. Sew the rows together to form the block. Press the final seams open. The block should measure 12½" x 12½". Repeat to make 20 blocks total, as shown.

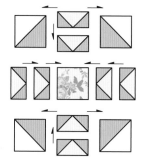

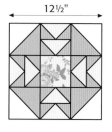

12½"

Make 4.   Make 4.

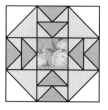 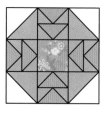

Make 4.   Make 4.

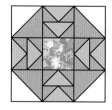

Make 4.

5. Sew the blocks from step 4 together in rows, as shown in the quilt diagram on page 58. Press the seams in opposite directions from row to row. Sew the rows together to form the quilt top.

6. Sew the 2½" x 4½" rectangles to the remaining flying-geese units in the combinations shown. Press toward the rectangles. Sew the half-square-triangle units to each side. Press toward the half-square-triangle units. Make a total of 18 of these units in the color combinations shown.

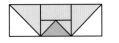

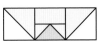

Make 2.

Make 2.

Make 2.

Make 2.

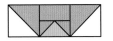

Make 2.

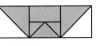

Make 2.

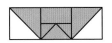

Make 1.

Make 1.

◆

Clever Tip

Make this quilt in flannel fat quarters for a cozy quilt to keep on the sofa.

◆

7. Sew the border units together in rows, as shown. Add half-square-triangle units to each end of the top and bottom borders.

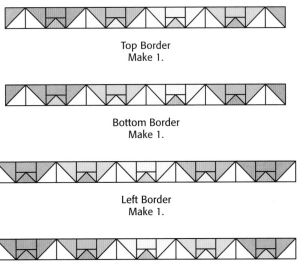

Top Border
Make 1.

Bottom Border
Make 1.

Left Border
Make 1.

Right Border
Make 1.

8. Sew the side borders to the quilt. Press. Sew the top and bottom borders to the quilt. Press.

9. Quilt as desired and bind. Refer to "Finishing Your Quilt" on page 21 for more details if needed.

SECRETS IN THE GARDEN RUNNER

Designed by Susan Teegarden Dissmore;
sewn and quilted by Lorri Gellerson, 2003.

Quilt Essentials

The block from "Secrets in the Garden" (page 54) is perfect for a table runner. When midnight inspiration for this table runner struck, I decided to make it in an entirely different color palette of rich, deep autumn shades.

MATERIALS

Yardages are based on 42"-wide fabric.

- ⅝ yard of a main print for the block centers and outer border
- 1 fat quarter of light beige for the block background
- 1 fat quarter *each* of green, gold, red, blue, and purple prints for the blocks*
- 1 yard of fabric for backing (or a 20" x 72" piece)
- ⅜ yard of fabric for binding
- 20" x 72" piece of batting

* *Or choose five colors that complement or coordinate with the main print.*

CUTTING

All measurements include ¼" seam allowances.

From *each* green, gold, and red print, cut:

- 1 strip, 5" x 21". Cut the strip into 2 squares, 4⅞" x 4⅞" and 4 rectangles, 2½" x 4½". Cut the squares in half diagonally once to yield 4 triangles.
- 4 strips, 2½" x 21". Cut the strips into 6 rectangles, 2½" x 4½", and 16 squares, 2½" x 2½".

From *each* blue and purple print, cut:

- 1 strip, 5" x 21". Cut the strip into 2 squares, 4⅞" x 4⅞", and 4 rectangles, 2½" x 4½". Cut the squares in half diagonally once to yield 4 triangles.
- 4 strips, 2½" x 21". Cut the strips into 7 rectangles, 2½" x 4½", and 16 squares, 2½" x 2½".

From the light beige, cut:

- 3 strips, 4⅞" x 21". Cut the strips into 10 squares, 4⅞" x 4⅞"; cut the squares in half diagonally once to yield 20 triangles.

From the main print, cut:

- 5 squares, 4½" x 4½"
- 1 strip, 8½" x 42". Cut the strip into 8 rectangles, 2½" x 8½", 4 rectangles, 2½" x 6½", and 4 rectangles, 2½" x 4½".
- 2 strips, 2½" x 42". Cut the strip into 24 squares, 2½" x 2½".

ASSEMBLY

1. Make flying-geese units in the color combinations and quantities shown using the 2½" squares and 2½" x 4½" rectangles. Refer to step 1 on page 55 for details if needed.

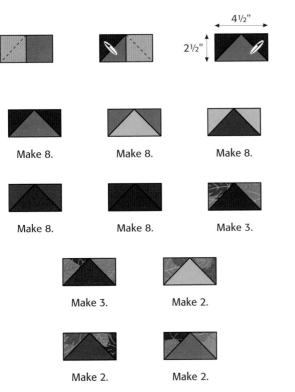

Make 8.   Make 8.   Make 8.

Make 8.   Make 8.   Make 3.

Make 3.   Make 2.

Make 2.   Make 2.

2. Make half-square-triangle units in the color combinations shown. You will need four of each.

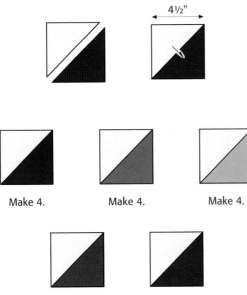

Make 4.   Make 4.   Make 4.

Make 4.   Make 4.

3. Using the units from steps 1 and 2 and the main print center squares, make the blocks as described in step 4 on page 56. You will need one of each color combination.

4. Sew the blocks together in one vertical row. Press.

5. Sew the main print rectangles to the remaining flying-geese units from step 1 to make the borders, as shown in the quilt diagram. Press toward the rectangles.

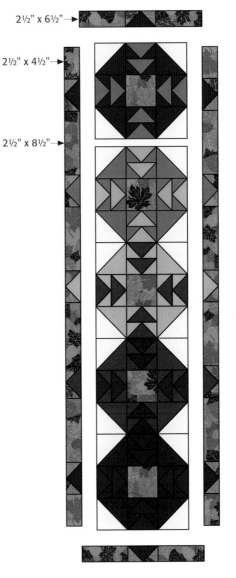

2½" x 6½"

2½" x 4½"

2½" x 8½"

6. Sew the side borders to the quilt. Press toward the borders. Sew the top and bottom borders to the quilt. Press toward the borders.

7. Quilt as desired and bind. Refer to "Finishing Your Quilt" on page 21 for more details if needed.

SUBTLE STARS

Designed and sewn by Susan Teegarden Dissmore; machine quilted by Eileen Peacher, 2003.

Quilt Essentials

Finished quilt: 90" x 114"
Finished block: 12" x 12"
Fat quarters: 61

A captivating collection of subtly colored prints inspired this quilt design. I designed blocks that, when rotated, would create a star pattern. The pieced outer borders complete unfinished star patterns and emphasize the mysterious, floating inner stars. The quilt keeps the viewer's eye entranced, roving over the quilt to find the stars, however fleeting they might be.

MATERIALS

Yardages are based on 42"-wide fabric.

- 12 fat quarters of assorted light beige tone-on-tone prints for blocks and inner border
- 10 fat quarters of assorted large-scale floral prints for the center of the diamond-in-a-square units
- 6 fat quarters of assorted beige small-scale floral prints for blocks and inner border
- 6 fat quarters of assorted blue tone-on-tone prints for blocks and outer border
- 5 fat quarters *each* of assorted green, yellow, and pink tone-on-tone prints for blocks and outer border
- 3 fat quarters *each* of assorted blue, pink, green, and yellow small-scale floral prints for blocks and inner border
- 9 yards of fabric for backing
- 1 yard of fabric for binding
- 98" x 120" piece of batting

CUTTING

All measurements include ¼" seam allowances.

From the 6 assorted blue tone-on-tone prints, cut:

- 14 strips, 3⅞" x 21". Cut the strips into a total of 68 squares, 3⅞" x 3⅞"; cut the squares in half diagonally once to yield 136 triangles.
- 9 strips, 3½" x 21". Reserve 7 strips; from the remaining strips, cut a total of 8 squares, 3½" x 3½".

From *each* set of 5 assorted green and yellow tone-on-tone prints, cut:

- 14 strips, 3⅞" x 21". Cut the strips into a total of 68 squares, 3⅞" x 3⅞"; cut the squares in half diagonally once to yield 136 triangles.
- 7 strips, 3½" x 21"

From the 5 assorted pink tone-on-tone prints, cut:

- 13 strips, 3⅞" x 21". Cut the strips into a total of 64 squares, 3⅞" x 3⅞"; cut the squares in half diagonally once to yield 128 triangles.
- 9 strips, 3½" x 21". Reserve 7 strips; from the remaining strips, cut a total of 8 squares, 3½" x 3½".

From the 10 assorted large-scale floral prints, selectively cut:

- 48 squares, 4¾" x 4¾" ("on point," if desired)

From the 12 assorted light beige tone-on-tone prints, cut:

- 43 strips, 3⅞" x 21". Cut the strips into 172 squares, 3⅞" x 3⅞"; cut the squares in half diagonally once to yield 344 triangles.

- 5 strips, 12½" x 21". Cut the strips into 14 rectangles, 12½" x 6½".

- 2 strips, 6½" x 21". Cut the strips into 4 squares, 6½" x 6½".

From *each* set of 3 assorted blue and pink small-scale floral prints, cut:

- 12 strips, 3½" x 21". Cut the strips into 56 squares, 3½" x 3½".

From the 6 assorted beige small-scale floral prints, cut:

- 25 strips, 3½" x 21". Cut the strips into 124 squares, 3½" x 3½".

From *each* set of 3 assorted green and yellow small-scale floral prints, cut:

- 11 strips, 3½" x 21". Cut the strips into 54 squares, 3½" x 3½".

Clever Tip

Although the diagrams show a specific color for the center of each diamond-in-a-square unit, feel free to change the colors to suit your preference.

ASSEMBLY

1. Sew the triangles cut from the blue, green, yellow, and pink tone-on-tone prints to each side of the large-scale floral squares to make the diamond-in-a-square units, as shown. Press toward the triangles and trim to 6½" x 6½".

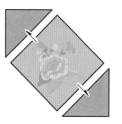
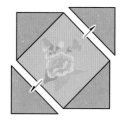

6½"

Make 12 with blue corners.

Make 12 with green corners.

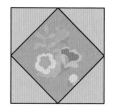

Make 12 with yellow corners.

Make 12 with pink corners.

2. Sew the remaining triangles cut from the blue, green, yellow, and pink tone-on-tone prints to the light beige triangles along their longest edges to form half-square-triangle units. Press toward the darker fabric and trim to 3½" x 3½".

4. Sew the units from steps 1 and 3 together in rows, as shown. Sew the rows together to form the blocks. Press as shown. Each block should measure 12½" x 12½". Press the final seam open.

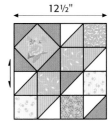

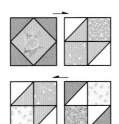

12½"

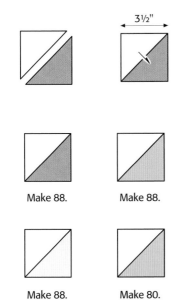

Make 88.   Make 88.

Make 88.   Make 80.

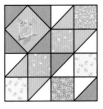

Make 12.   Make 12.

3. Sew the squares cut from the beige small-scale floral and assorted small-scale floral prints to the half-square-triangle units from step 2 to form four-patch units, as shown. Press toward the squares. Press the center seams, as shown.

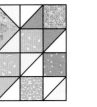

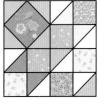

Make 12.   Make 12.

Make 12.   Make 12.   Make 12.   Make 12.

Make 12.   Make 12.   Make 12.   Make 12.

Make 12.   Make 12.   Make 12.   Make 12.

5. Arrange the blocks from step 4 into rows, as shown. Sew the rows together to form the quilt top. Press the rows in opposite directions.

6. Sew the squares cut from the light beige and small-scale floral prints to the remaining half-square-triangle units from step 2 to form the half-star blocks. Press in the opposite direction of the quilt top blocks.

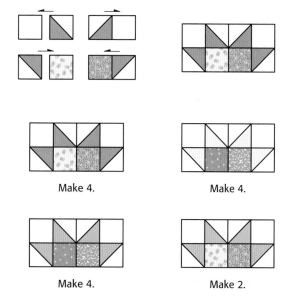

Make 4.   Make 4.

Make 4.   Make 2.

7. Sew the beige tone-on-tone 12½" x 6½" rectangles and the beige 6½" x 6½" squares to the ends of the half-star blocks to form the outer border units. Press toward the beige.

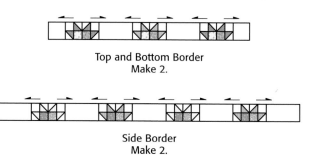

Top and Bottom Border
Make 2.

Side Border
Make 2.

8. Sew the shorter border units to the top and bottom of the quilt top. Press as desired. Sew the longer border units to the sides of the quilt top. Press as desired.

9. Sew the 3½" x 21" strips cut from the blue, green, yellow, and pink tone-on-tone prints into seven strip sets of four strips each. Press in one direction and crosscut into 33 segments, 3½" wide.

3½"

Make 7 strip sets.
Cut 33 segments.

10. Sew the crosscut segments from step 9 end to end to form one long strip. Count off 30 squares and "unsew" to make the top border. Count off 36 squares for the right side border, 30 squares for the bottom border, and 36 squares for the left side border, in that order. Press as you go. Re-press where necessary.

11. Sew the side borders to the quilt first. Press. Sew the top and bottom borders to the quilt. Press.

12. Quilt as desired and bind. Refer to "Finishing Your Quilt" on page 21 for more details if needed.

SUSAN'S SUBTLE STARS

Designed and sewn by Susan Teegarden Dissmore; machine quilted by Eileen Peacher, 2003.

Quilt Essentials

Finished quilt: 66" x 90"
Finished block: 12" x 12"
Fat quarters: 39

This quilt is essentially the same as "Subtle Stars" (page 62), but smaller. After making the larger quilt, I wanted a smaller version. I just happened to have another collection of fat quarters in my fabric closet that was perfect for this design! When I reached the outer border, I discovered that I didn't have enough of my four striped fabrics for larger rectangles, so I changed the cuts to squares. The alternating stripes are a pleasant complement to the floral prints.

MATERIALS

Yardages are based on 42"-wide fabric.

- 6 fat quarters of assorted light beige prints for blocks and inner border
- 5 fat quarters of assorted floral prints for the center of the diamond-in-a-square units
- 4 fat quarters of assorted stripes for inner border
- 3 fat quarters *each* of assorted dark prints in blue, red, gold, and green for blocks and outer border
- 2 fat quarters *each* of assorted medium-light prints in blue, green, pink, and yellow for blocks and inner border
- 1 fat quarter *each* of medium-dark prints in blue, green, and pink for diamond-in-a-square units
- 1 fat quarter of medium-dark yellow print for diamond-in-a-square units and inner border
- 5½ yards of fabric for backing
- ¾ yard of fabric for binding
- 74" x 98" piece of batting

CUTTING

All measurements include ¼" seam allowances.

From *each* medium-dark blue, green, and pink print, cut:

- 3 strips, 3⅞" x 21". Cut the strips into 12 squares, 3⅞" x 3⅞"; cut the squares in half diagonally once to yield 24 triangles.

From the medium-dark yellow print, cut:

- 3 strips, 3⅞" x 21". Cut the strips into 12 squares, 3⅞" x 3⅞"; cut the squares in half diagonally once to yield 24 triangles.
- 1 strip, 3½" x 21". Cut the strip into 4 squares, 3½" x 3½".

From the 5 assorted floral prints, selectively cut a total of:

- 24 squares, 4¾" x 4¾"

From *each* of the 3 assorted dark blue, red, and gold prints, cut:

- 2 strips, 3⅞" x 21". Cut the strips into 8 squares, 3⅞" x 3⅞"; cut the squares in half diagonally once to yield 16 triangles (a total of 48 triangles per color with 4 extra per color).
- 2 strips, 3½" x 21"

From *each* of the 3 assorted dark green prints, cut:

- 2 strips, 3⅞" x 21". Cut the strips into 9 squares, 3⅞" x 3⅞"; cut the squares in half diagonally once to yield 18 triangles (a total of 54 triangles, with 2 extra).
- 2 strips, 3½" x 21"

From *each* of 4 light beige prints, cut:

- 4 strips, 3⅞" x 21". Cut the strips into 18 squares, 3⅞" x 3⅞"; cut the squares in half diagonally once to yield 36 triangles (a total of 144).

From 2 light beige prints, cut a total of:

- 4 strips, 3⅞" x 21". Cut the strips into 20 squares, 3⅞" x 3⅞"; cut the squares in half diagonally once to yield 40 triangles.
- 4 strips, 3½" x 21". Cut the strips into 20 squares, 3½" x 3½".

From *each* of 2 medium-light blue, green, pink, and yellow prints, cut:

- 4 strips, 3½" x 21". Cut the strips into 20 squares, 3½" x 3½" (a total of 40 per color).

From *each* of the 4 assorted stripes, cut:

- 2 strips, 6½" x 21". Cut the strips into 6 squares, 6½" x 6½" (a total of 24).

Clever Tip

To make this quilt guy-friendly, use sporting theme prints accented with plaid triangles for the diamond-in-a-square units. Then choose dark and medium-light prints that coordinate with the main theme prints.

ASSEMBLY

1. Sew the triangles cut from the medium-dark blue, green, pink, and yellow prints to each side of the floral squares to make the diamond-in-a-square units, as shown. Press toward the triangles and trim to 6½" x 6½".

6½"

Make 6.   Make 6.

Make 6.   Make 6.

2. Sew the triangles cut from the dark blue, red, gold, and green to the triangles cut from the light beige prints along their longest edges to form half-square triangle units. Press toward the dark fabric and trim to 3½" x 3½".

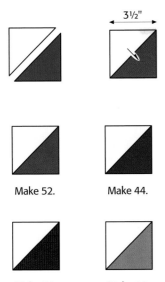

3½"

Make 52.   Make 44.

Make 44.   Make 44.

3. Sew the squares cut from the medium-light blue, green, pink, and yellow prints to the half-square triangle units from step 2 to form four-patch units, as shown. Press toward the square. Press the center seams as shown.

3½"

Make 6.   Make 6.   Make 6.   Make 6.

Make 6.   Make 6.   Make 6.   Make 6.

Make 6.   Make 6.   Make 6.   Make 6.

4. Sew the units from step 1 and step 3 together in rows. Sew the rows together to form the block. Press as shown. Each block should measure 12½" x 12½". Press the final seam open.

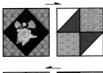

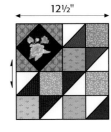

12½"

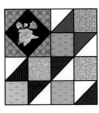   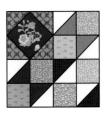

Make 6.   Make 6.

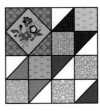   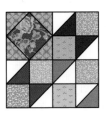

Make 6.   Make 6.

71

5. Arrange the blocks from step 4 into rows, as shown. Sew the blocks together into rows. Press the rows in opposite directions. Sew the rows together to form the quilt top.

6. Sew the squares cut from the light beige and medium-light prints to the remaining half-square-triangle units from step 2 to form the half-star blocks. Press in the opposite direction of the quilt top blocks.

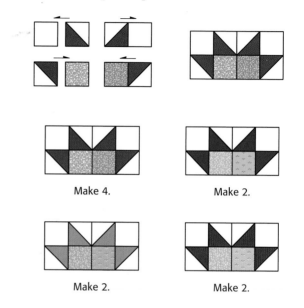

Make 4.   Make 2.

Make 2.   Make 2.

7. Sew the 6½" x 6½" striped squares to the half-star units to form the inner border, as shown in the quilt diagram. Press toward the squares.

8. Sew the top and bottom borders to the quilt top. Press toward the borders. Sew the remaining borders to each side. Press toward the borders.

9. Sew the 3½" x 21" strips cut from the dark blue, red, gold, and green prints into 6 strip sets of 4 strips each. Press in one direction and crosscut into 25 segments, 3½" wide.

3½"

Make 6 strip sets.
Cut 25 segments.

10. Sew the crosscut segments from step 9 end to end to form one long strip. Count off 22 squares and "unsew" to make the top border. Count off 28 squares for the right side border, 22 squares for the bottom border, and 28 squares for the left side border, in that order. Press as you go. Re-press where necessary.

11. Sew the side borders to the quilt. Press toward the outer border. Sew the top and bottom borders to the quilt. Press.

12. Quilt as desired and bind. Refer to "Finishing Your Quilt" on page 21 for more details if needed.

SUMMER AT AUNT JANE'S

Designed and sewn by Susan Teegarden Dissmore; machine quilted by Eileen Peacher, 2001.

Quilt Essentials

Finished quilt: 60" x 76"
Finished block: 8" x 8"
Fat quarters: 28

The Kansas Troubles block is one of my favorites, when I can get past the thought of sewing all the half-square triangles needed! For this quilt I persevered, however, and went above and beyond the blocks. The charming prints in green, gold, blue, and pink inspired me to make even more half-square triangles for the pieced borders. It's not difficult at all, but it's good motivation to focus on accurate cutting and piecing. Go for it…it's worth it!

MATERIALS

Yardages are based on 42"-wide fabric.

- 12 fat quarters of assorted medium, medium-light, and medium-dark prints in green, pink, blue, and yellow
- 8 fat quarters of assorted light prints
- 8 fat quarters of assorted dark prints in green, pink, and blue
- 1 yard medium blue for inner border
- 4¾ yards of fabric for backing
- ¾ yard of fabric for binding
- 68" x 84" piece of batting

CUTTING

All measurements include ¼" seam allowances.

From the 8 light prints, cut a total of:

- 8 strips, 2½" x 21". Cut the strips into 52 squares, 2½" x 2½".
- 36 strips, 2⅞" x 21". Cut the strips into 212 squares, 2⅞" x 2⅞"; cut the squares in half diagonally once to yield 424 triangles.

From the 8 dark prints, cut a total of:

- 44 strips, 2⅞" x 21". Cut the strips into 260 squares, 2⅞" x 2⅞"; cut the squares in half diagonally once to yield 520 triangles.
- 4 squares, 2½" x 2½".

From *each* of the 12 medium prints, cut:

- 1 strip, 8⅞" x 21". Cut the strip into 2 squares, 8⅞" x 8⅞"; cut the squares in half diagonally once to yield 4 triangles.
- 1 strip, 4⅞" x 21". Cut the strip into 2 squares, 4⅞" x 4⅞"; cut the squares in half diagonally once to yield 4 triangles.

From the medium blue, cut:

- 8 strips, 2½" x length of fabric (36")
- 4 rectangles, 2½" x 4½"
- 4 rectangles, 2½" x 6½"

ASSEMBLY

1. Using the 2⅞" triangles, sew the light print triangles to the dark print triangles along their longest edges to form half-square-triangle units. Press the seams toward the dark triangles. Trim the dog ears and make sure units measure 2½" x 2½". Note that in the quilt shown, each block uses identical units, so you may want to make your units in sets of four. In addition, reserve two dark triangles per block; do not sew these into half-square-triangle units.

2½"

Make 424.

2. Sew 192 of the half-square-triangle units from step 1 together in pairs. Make 48 pairs with the triangles pointing right and 48 pairs with the triangles pointing left. Press the seams toward the dark triangle.

Make 48.

Make 48.

3. Sew a dark print triangle to one end of each of the pairs, as shown. Press toward the dark triangle.

Make 48.

Make 48.

4. Sew 48 of the units from step 3 to one side of the 4⅞" medium print triangles. Press the seams toward the large triangle.

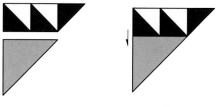

Make 48.

5. Sew the 2½" light print squares to the ends of the 48 remaining units from step 3. Press the seams toward the squares.

Make 48.

6. Sew the units from steps 4 and 5 together, as shown. Press the seams toward the large triangles.

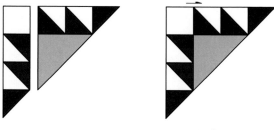

Make 48.

7. Sew the units from step 6 to the 8⅞" medium print triangles. Press the seams toward the large triangles and trim the completed blocks to 8½" x 8½".

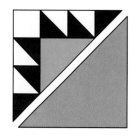 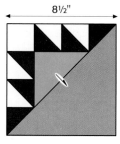

8½"

Make 48.

8. Arrange the blocks from step 7 into groups of four, as shown. For each unit, sew the blocks together in rows. Press the seams toward the large triangles. Sew the rows together to make the four-block units. Press the final seams of half the units in one direction, and the other half in the opposite direction.

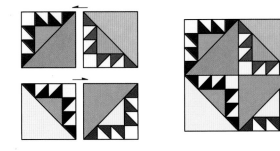

Clever Tip

Prior to sewing the blocks together into groups of four, arrange them on a design wall or other surface to determine the desired color placement. Then sew the four-block units together row by row, pressing as you sew them together.

9. Sew the four-block units from step 8 together in rows. Press the rows in opposite directions. Sew the rows together to form the quilt top. Press the seams in one direction.

10. Using eight half-square-triangle units from step 1 and the four light and four dark 2½" squares, make Four Patch blocks as shown. Press the seams toward the squares. Press the final seams as desired.

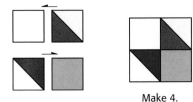

Make 4.

11. Sew the medium blue rectangles to each side of the Four Patch block from step 10. Press the seams toward the medium blue fabric. Each block should measure 6½" x 6½".

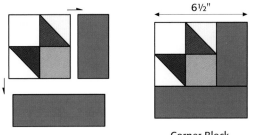

Corner Block
Make 4.

12. Sew the remaining half-square-triangle units from step 1 into pairs, as shown. Press all seams in one direction.

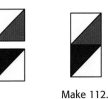

Make 112.

13. Alternating the colors, sew 24 of the pairs from step 12 together to form one long row, as shown in the quilt diagram. (Note: To make seams easy to butt together, simply rotate units as needed so seams are pressed in opposite directions.) Press seams in one direction and repeat using another 24 pairs. Make two more borders using 32 pairs for each.

14. Sew the 2½" x 36" medium blue strips together end to end in pairs to make four long strips. Press.

15. Cut two strips from step 14 to 48½". Referring to the quilt diagram on page 78, sew these strips to one side of the set of 24 pairs of half-square-triangle units. Press the seams toward the strips. Sew the blocks from step 11 to each end. Press the seams toward the half-square triangles.

16. Cut the remaining two inner-border strips from step 14 to 64½". Referring to the quilt diagram, sew the strips to one side of the remaining two sets of half-square-triangle units. Press the seams toward the strips.

17. Sew the side border units from step 16 to the quilt top. Press the seams toward the blue strips.

18. Sew the top and bottom border units from step 15 to the quilt top. Press the seams toward the blue strips.

19. Quilt as desired and bind. Refer to "Finishing Your Quilt" on page 21 for more details if needed.

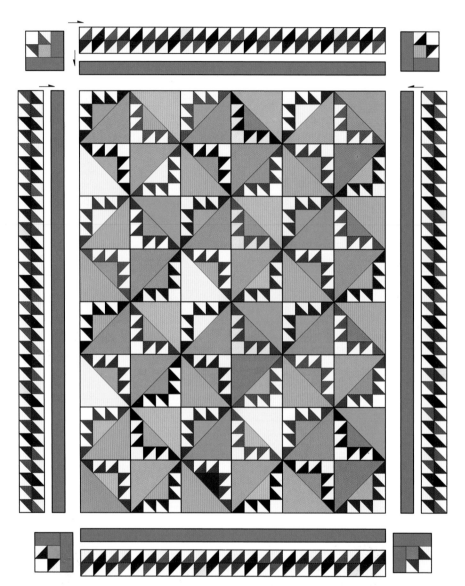

SUMMER COTTAGE NINE PATCH

Designed and sewn by Susan Teegarden Dissmore; machine quilted by Eileen Peacher, 1999.

Quilt Essentials

Finished quilt: 84" x 96"
Finished block: 6" x 6"
Fat quarters: 56

Here's an easy bed-size quilt to make totally out of fat quarters. This was the first quilt I designed using a large fat-quarter bundle. I wanted to create a quilt that was strip-pieced and simple. While I love the floral cottage look, using different fabrics and a different color palette will give this queen-size quilt a totally different look. I kept all of the scraps and pieced them together Crazy quilt–style to create coordinating pillow covers.

MATERIALS

Yardages are based on 42"-wide fabric.

- 12 fat quarters of assorted light beige prints for the first and third borders
- 11 fat quarters of assorted large-scale floral prints for the square blocks
- 11 fat quarters of assorted medium-scale floral prints for the Nine Patch blocks
- 11 fat quarters of assorted medium-scale prints for the Nine Patch blocks
- 11 fat quarters of assorted medium or dark tone-on-tone prints for the second border
- 7¾ yards of fabric for backing
- ⅞ yard of fabric for binding
- 92" x 104" piece of batting

CUTTING

All measurements include ¼" seam allowances.

From *each* of the 11 medium-scale floral prints, cut:

- 6 strips, 2½" x 21"

From *each* of the 11 medium-scale prints, cut:

- 6 strips, 2½" x 21"

From *each* of the 11 large-scale floral prints, selectively cut:

- 4 squares, 6½" x 6½" (4 extra squares)

From *each* of the 12 light beige prints, cut:

- 4 strips, 3½" x 21"

From *each* of the 11 medium or dark tone-on-tone prints, cut:

- 6 strips, 2½" x 21"

ASSEMBLY

1. To make the Nine Patch blocks, sew three medium-scale floral strips and three medium-scale print strips together to form strip sets A and B. Press strip set A toward the outer strips and strip set B toward the center strip. Crosscut the strip sets into 120 segments, 2½" wide.

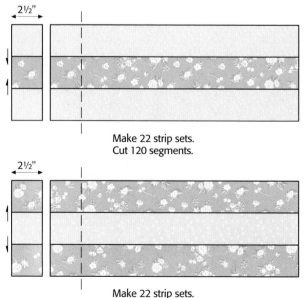

Make 22 strip sets.
Cut 120 segments.

Make 22 strip sets.
Cut 120 segments.

2. Sew the crosscut segments from step 1 together to form the Nine Patch blocks. Press as desired. Each block should measure 6½" x 6½". Make a total of 80 Nine Patch blocks.

Make 40.

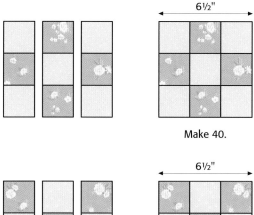

Make 40.

3. Sew the 6½" squares cut from the large-scale floral prints and the Nine Patch blocks together to form the center section of the quilt. Press the seams in opposite directions from row to row. Sew the rows together. Press all the seams in one direction.

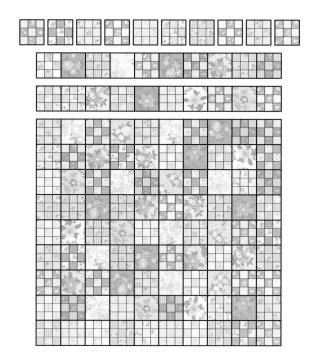

4. Sew twelve of the 3½"-wide light beige strips together into a strip set. Repeat to make four strip sets. Press the seams in one direction. Crosscut each strip set into five segments, 3½" wide.

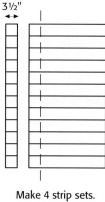

Make 4 strip sets.
Cut 20 segments.

5. Sew two crosscut segments from step 4 together end to end to form one long strip. Remove four squares, leaving a total of 20 squares for the top border. Press. Repeat to make a second strip for the bottom border. Align the strips with the quilt top and re-press seams in the opposite direction where necessary. Sew the border units to the top and bottom of the quilt. Press the seams toward the border.

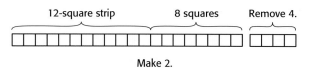

Make 2.

6. Sew two crosscut segments from step 4 together end to end to form one long strip. Add two of the squares removed in step 5, making a total of 26 squares. Press. Repeat to make a second strip. Align the strips with the quilt top and re-press seams in the opposite direction where necessary. Sew the border units to the sides of the quilt. Press the seams toward the borders.

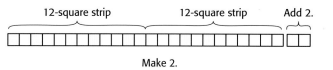

Make 2.

7. Sew the medium or dark tone-on-tone strips into 22 strip sets of three strips each. Crosscut the strip sets into 156 segments, 2½" wide. Press.

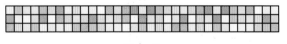

Make 22 strip sets.
Cut 156 segments.

Clever Tip

Each of the three strips in the 22 strip sets should be different in both color and scale to create a scrappy border. The pressing direction will depend on the final layout of the crosscut units. Before pressing and crosscutting the strip sets, lay them out in an order that is pleasing to you. Press the first strip set in one direction. Press the next strip set in the opposite direction. Continue pressing in the same manner until all strip sets are pressed. Crosscut the strip sets and keep them in their appropriate sewing order.

8. Sew 33 crosscut segments together side by side. Press in the opposite direction of the inner border. Sew these border units to the top and bottom of the quilt. Press.

Make 2.

9. Sew 45 crosscut segments together side by side. Press in the opposite direction of the inner border. Sew these border units to the sides of the quilt. Press as desired.

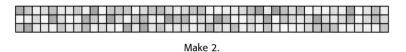

Make 2.

10. Sew three crosscut segments from step 4 together end to end to form one long strip. Remove 10 squares, leaving a total of 26 squares. Align the strip with the top of the quilt and press seams in the opposite direction of the second inner border. Repeat to make a second border strip. Sew these border units to the top and bottom of the quilt. Press as desired.

11. Sew three crosscut segments from step 4 together end to end to form one long strip. Remove four squares, leaving a total of 32 squares. Align the strip with the side of the quilt top and press seams in the opposite direction of the second inner border. Repeat to make a second border strip. Sew these border units to the sides of the quilt. Press as desired.

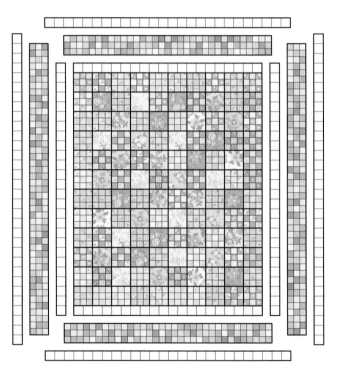

12. Quilt as desired and bind. Refer to "Finishing Your Quilt" on page 21 for more details if needed.

WINTER CELEBRATION NINE PATCH

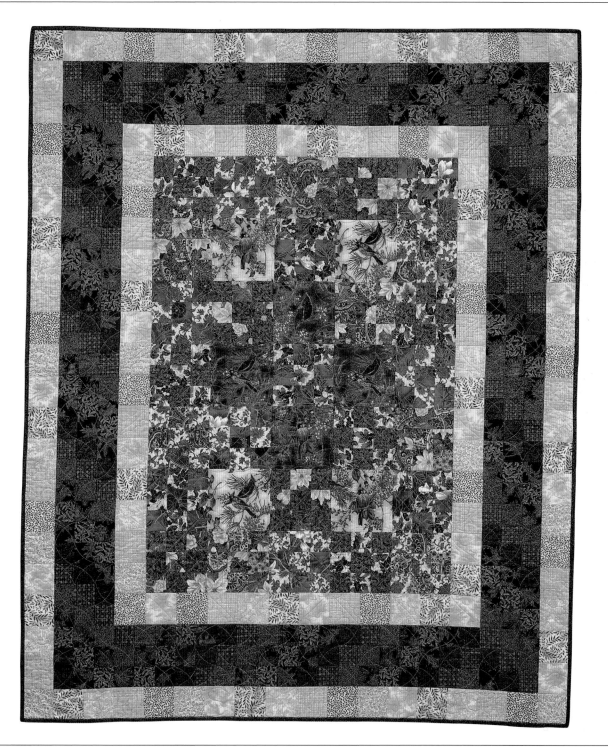

Designed and sewn by Susan Teegarden Dissmore; machine quilted by Sue Gantt, 2003.

Quilt Essentials

Finished quilt: 54" x 66"
Finished block: 6" x 6"
Fat quarters: 21

Here's a midwinter version of "Summer Cottage Nine Patch" on page 79. I like to have smaller lap-size quilts, and this one is especially nice during the holidays. During the Christmas season there are so many beautiful holiday prints to chose from; they run the gamut from elegant to whimsical. Almost any of these seasonal prints would be suitable for this easy Nine Patch design. I chose two cardinal prints for the main blocks and accented them with fabrics in the same colors.

MATERIALS

Yardages are based on 42"-wide fabric.

- 7 fat quarters of assorted light beige prints for the first and third borders
- 6 fat quarters of assorted dark tone-on-tone prints for the second border
- 3 fat quarters of assorted medium-scale floral prints for the Nine Patch blocks
- 3 fat quarters of assorted medium-scale prints for the Nine Patch blocks
- 2 fat quarters of holiday-theme prints for the square blocks
- 3½ yards of fabric for backing
- ⅞ yard of fabric for binding
- 62" x 74" piece of batting

CUTTING

All measurements include ¼" seam allowances.

From *each* of the 3 medium-scale floral prints, cut:

- 6 strips, 2½" x 21"

From *each* of the 3 medium-scale prints, cut:

- 6 strips, 2½" x 21"

From *each* of the 2 holiday-theme prints, selectively cut:

- 4 squares, 6½" x 6½"

From *each* of the 7 light beige prints, cut:

- 4 strips, 3½" x 21"

From *each* of the 6 dark tone-on-tone prints, cut:

- 6 strips, 2½" x 21"

ASSEMBLY

1. Arrange the medium-scale floral strips and medium-scale print strips to form strip sets A and B. Sew together; press strip set A toward the outer strips and strip set B toward the center strip. Crosscut each strip set into eight 2½" segments. You will have extras.

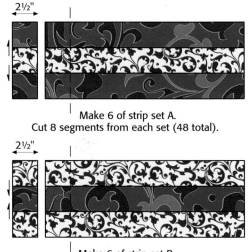

Make 6 of strip set A.
Cut 8 segments from each set (48 total).

Make 6 of strip set B.
Cut 8 segments from each set (48 total).

2. Sew the crosscut segments from strip sets A and B in step 1 together to form the Nine Patch blocks. Press. Each block should measure 6½" x 6½". Make a total of 27 Nine Patch blocks, as shown.

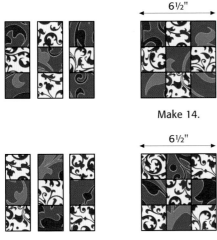

Make 14.

Make 13.

3. Sew the 6½" squares cut from the holiday-theme print and the Nine Patch blocks together to form the center section of the quilt, as shown. Press the seams in opposite directions from row to row. Sew the rows together. Press the seams in one direction.

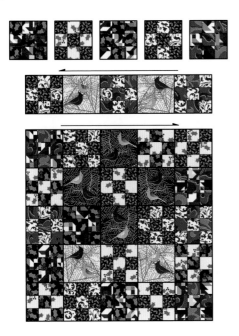

4. Sew seven of the 3½"-wide light beige strips together into a strip set. Repeat to make four strip sets. Press the seams in one direction. Crosscut each strip set into five segments, 3½" wide.

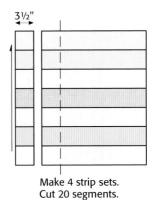

Make 4 strip sets.
Cut 20 segments.

5. Sew two crosscut segments from step 4 together end to end to form one long strip for the top border. Remove 4 squares, leaving a total of 10 squares. Press. Repeat for the bottom border. Re-press seams in the opposite direction of the quilt top where necessary. Sew the border units to the top and bottom of the quilt. Press toward the border.

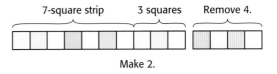

Make 2.

6. Sew two crosscut segments from step 4 together end to end to form one long strip for the side border. Add two squares removed in step 5, making a total of 16 squares. Press. Repeat for the second side. Re-press seams in the opposite direction of the quilt top where necessary. Sew the border units to the sides of the quilt. Press toward the border.

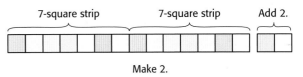

Make 2.

7. Sew the dark tone-on-tone strips into 12 strip sets of three strips each as shown. Crosscut each strip set into 8 segments, 2½" wide, for a total of 96.

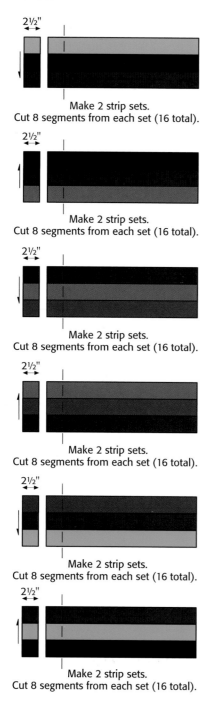

2½"

Make 2 strip sets.
Cut 8 segments from each set (16 total).

2½"

Make 2 strip sets.
Cut 8 segments from each set (16 total).

2½"

Make 2 strip sets.
Cut 8 segments from each set (16 total).

2½"

Make 2 strip sets.
Cut 8 segments from each set (16 total).

2½"

Make 2 strip sets.
Cut 8 segments from each set (16 total).

2½"

Make 2 strip sets.
Cut 8 segments from each set (16 total).

8. For the top border, arrange 18 segments sequentially as shown to create a diagonal pattern. Sew the segments together side by side. Press in the opposite direction of the inner border. Repeat for the bottom border.

Sew these border units to the top and bottom of the quilt. Press toward the darker border.

Make 2.

9. Sew 30 segments together as shown for the side border. Press in the opposite direction of the inner border. Repeat. Sew these border units to the sides of the quilt. Press.

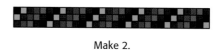

Make 2.

10. Sew three light beige crosscut segments from step 4 together end to end to form one long strip. Remove 5 of the squares, leaving a total of 16 squares. Press in the opposite direction of the second inner border and repeat. Sew these border units to the top and bottom of the quilt. Press.

11. Sew three of the remaining light beige crosscut segments together end to end to form one long strip. Add one of the squares removed in step 10 to each strip, for a total of 22 squares. Press in the opposite direction of the second inner border. Repeat. Sew these border units to the sides of the quilt. Press.

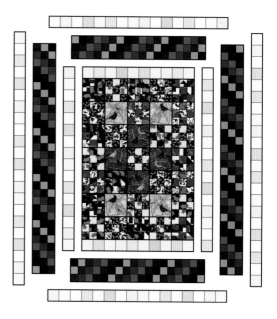

12. Quilt as desired and bind. Refer to "Finishing Your Quilt" on page 21 for more details if needed.

TEA TIME TABLE TOPPER

Designed, sewn, and quilted by Susan Teegarden Dissmore, 2002.

Quilt Essentials

Finished quilt: 30" x 30"

Finished block: 10" x 10"

Fat quarters: 7

I enjoy using my smaller quilts as table toppers in the kitchen and dining room. The teapot fabric and coordinating floral prints, toile prints, and plaids are ideal for this small table topper quilt. Use your favorite theme print and make a different one for every season or holiday!

MATERIALS

Yardages are based on 42"-wide fabric.

- 1 fat quarter of a teapot-theme print for the block centers
- 1 fat quarter each of burgundy, white-and-green print, yellow, medium pink toile, medium green floral, and dark green floral for the blocks and borders
- 1 yard of fabric for backing
- ⅜ yard of fabric for binding
- 36" x 36" piece of batting

CUTTING

All measurements include ¼" seam allowances.

From the burgundy, cut:

- 4 squares, 6¼" x 6¼"; cut the squares in half diagonally twice to yield 16 triangles.
- 8 squares, 3⅜" x 3⅜"; cut the squares in half diagonally once to yield 16 triangles.

From the white-and-green, cut:

- 2 strips, 3⅜" x 21". Cut the strips into 8 squares, 3⅜" x 3⅜"; cut the squares in half diagonally once to yield 16 triangles.
- 1 square, 6¼" x 6¼"; cut the square in half diagonally twice to yield 4 triangles.
- 4 rectangles, 3" x 5½"

From the yellow, cut:

- 4 strips, 3⅜" x 21". Cut the strips into 16 squares, 3⅜" x 3⅜"; cut the squares in half diagonally once to yield 32 triangles.

From the medium pink toile, cut:

- 4 squares, 6¼" x 6¼"; cut the squares in half diagonally twice to yield 16 triangles.

From the teapot-theme print, selectively cut:

- 4 squares, 5½" x 5½"

From *each* medium and dark green floral, cut:

- 1 square, 6¼" x 6¼"; cut the square in half diagonally twice to yield 4 triangles.
- 2 rectangles, 3" x 5½"
- 4 squares, 3⅜" x 3⅜"; cut the squares in half diagonally once to yield 8 triangles.
- 14 squares, 3" x 3"

ASSEMBLY

1. Using the triangles cut from the 3⅜" squares, sew a burgundy triangle to a white-and-green triangle along their long edges. Press toward the dark pink and trim to 3" x 3". Make 16 half-square triangle units.

Make 16.

2. With right sides together, sew a yellow triangle to one side of a medium pink toile triangle. Press toward the pink. Repeat on the other side. Press and trim to 3" x 5½". Make 16 flying-geese units.

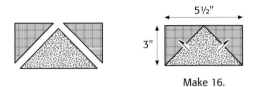

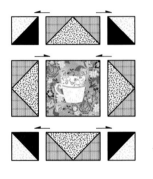

Make 16.

3. Sew the units from steps 1 and 2 and the teapot-theme print squares together in rows, as shown. Press. Sew the rows together to form the block. Press. Make four blocks. Each block should measure 10½" x 10½".

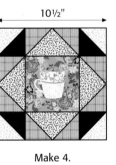

10½"

Make 4.

4. Using the triangles cut from the 6¼" squares, sew a burgundy triangle to a dark green floral triangle along the shortest edge. Press toward the burgundy. Repeat using a burgundy and a white-and-green triangle. Sew the units together. Press and trim to 5½" x 5½". Make two hourglass units.

5½"

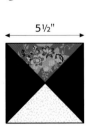

Make 2.

5. Repeat step 4 using the burgundy, dark green floral, medium green floral, and white-and-green triangles, as shown. Press toward the darker fabrics.

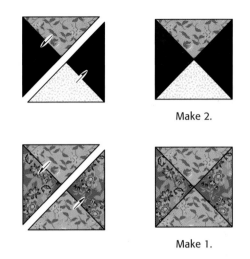

Make 2.

Make 1.

6. Using the units from steps 4 and 5 and the 3" x 5½" rectangles from the white-and-green, medium green floral, and dark green floral, sew the sashing sections together, as shown.

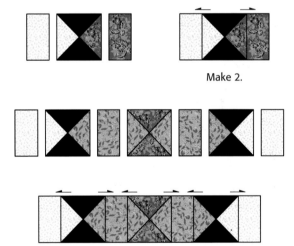

Make 2.

Make 1.

89

7. With right sides together, sew the long side of a dark green floral triangle to the left side of a burgundy triangle. Press toward the dark green floral. Repeat on the other side, using a medium green floral triangle. Press and trim to 3" x 5½". Repeat to make four.

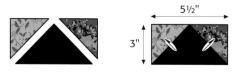

Make 4.

8. With right sides together, sew the long side of a medium green floral triangle to the left side of a burgundy triangle. Press toward the medium green floral. Repeat on the other side, using a dark green floral triangle. Press and trim to 3" x 5½". Repeat to make four.

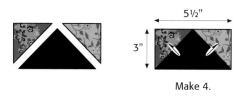

Make 4.

9. Sew the units from steps 7 and 8 and the medium and dark green 3" squares together in rows, as shown. Press as shown.

10. Sew the blocks from step 3 to the sashing units from step 6 to form the quilt top. Press the seams as shown.

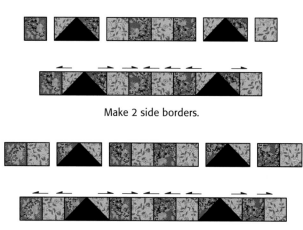

Make 2 side borders.

Make a top and a bottom border.

11. Sew the side borders to the quilt. Press toward the borders. Sew the top and bottom borders to the quilt. Press.

12. Quilt and bind as desired. Refer to "Finishing Your Quilt" on page 21 for more details if needed.

Clever Tip

Make this table topper and a matching table runner using the pattern beginning on the opposite page. Buy extra theme fabric to make coordinating napkins for a complete tea time ensemble.

TEA TIME
TABLE RUNNER

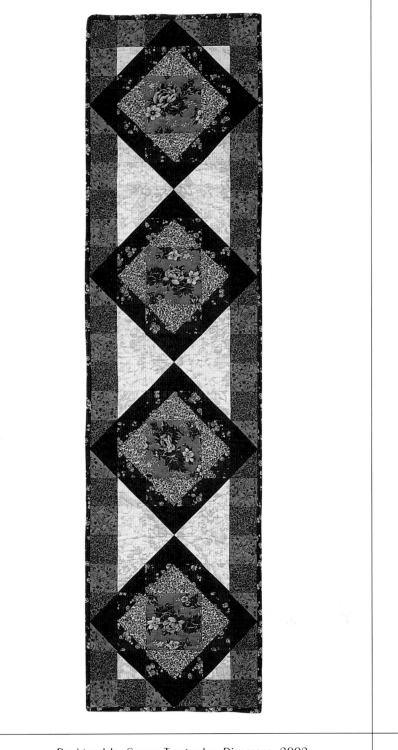

Designed by Susan Teegarden Dissmore, 2002.
Sewn and quilted by Stephanie Swensson, 2003.

Quilt Essentials

Finished quilt: 15" x 60"

Finished block: 10" x 10"

Fat quarters: 7

Table runners are a treat to sew, either for yourself or as a gift. They go together quickly and can make a bold decorating statement. Using fat quarters from a Christmas collection of red and green, we made the same four blocks as in "Tea Time Table Topper" on page 87 and set them in a vertical row to create a table runner with a completely different look. Have fun picking fat quarters with a holiday theme, a kitchen theme, a food theme—or just pick your favorite fabrics and start sewing!

MATERIALS

Yardages are based on 42"-wide fabric.

- 1 fat quarter of theme print for the block center
- 1 fat quarter *each* of dark red, medium red, and beige for the blocks and border
- 1 fat quarter *each* of two medium greens and one dark green for the blocks and border
- 1½ yards of fabric for backing (or a 23" x 68" piece)
- ½ yard of fabric for binding
- 23" x 68" piece of batting

CUTTING

All measurements include ¼" seam allowances.

From the dark red, cut:

- 4 squares, 6¼" x 6¼"; cut the squares in half diagonally twice to yield 16 triangles.
- 8 squares, 3⅜" x 3⅜"; cut the squares in half diagonally once to yield 16 triangles.

From the beige, cut:

- 2 strips, 3⅜" x 21". Cut the strips into 8 squares, 3⅜" x 3⅜", and 1 rectangle, 3" x 5½". Cut the squares in half diagonally once to yield 16 triangles.
- 2 squares, 6¼" x 6¼"; cut the squares in half diagonally twice to yield 8 triangles (2 extra).
- 5 rectangles, 3" x 5½"

From the medium red, cut:

- 3 strips, 3⅜" x 21". Cut the strips into 16 squares, 3⅜" x 3⅜"; cut the squares in half diagonally once to yield 32 triangles.

From 1 medium green, cut:

- 4 squares, 6¼" x 6¼"; cut the squares in half diagonally twice to yield 16 triangles.

From the theme print, selectively cut:

- 4 squares, 5½" x 5½"

From *each* of the second medium green and dark green, cut:

- 1 strip, 3⅜" x 21". Cut the strip into 5 squares, 3⅜" x 3⅜"; cut the squares in half diagonally once to yield 10 triangles.
- 3 strips, 3" x 21". Cut the strips into 18 squares, 3" x 3".

ASSEMBLY

1. Using the triangles cut from the 3⅜" squares, sew a dark red triangle to a beige triangle along their longest edges. Press toward the dark red and trim to 3" x 3". Make 16 half-square-triangle units.

Make 16.

2. With right sides together, sew a medium red triangle to one side of a medium green triangle cut from the 6¼" squares. Press toward the red. Repeat on the other side. Press and trim to 3" x 5½". Make 16 flying-geese units.

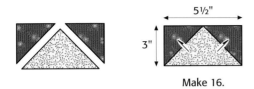

Make 16.

3. Sew the units from steps 1 and 2 and the theme print squares together in rows, and press as shown. Sew the rows together to form the block. Press. Make four blocks. Each block should measure 10½" x 10½".

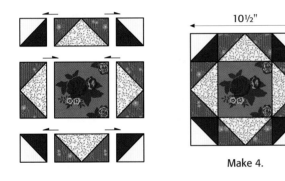

10½"

Make 4.

4. Sew the dark red triangles cut from the 6¼" squares to the beige triangles cut from the 6¼" squares, as shown. Press toward the red. Sew the units together to make three Hourglass blocks. Trim to 5½" x 5½".

5½"

Make 3.

5. Sew a 3" x 5½" beige rectangle to each side of the units from step 4. Make three sashing units.

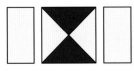

Make 3.

6. Sew medium green and dark green triangles to the dark red triangles, as shown, to make 10 flying-geese units. Press and trim to 3" x 5½".

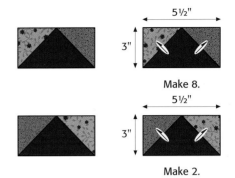

5½"

3"

Make 8.

5½"

3"

Make 2.

7. Using the flying-geese units and the 3" squares cut from the medium and dark green prints, sew the border units together in rows, as shown in the quilt diagram. Press opposite of the blocks.

8. Sew the blocks to the sashing units to form the quilt top. Press the seams open.

9. Sew the top and bottom borders to the quilt. Press as desired. Sew the side borders to the quilt. Press as desired.

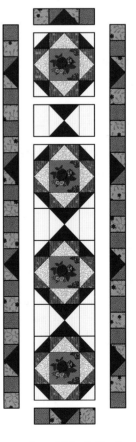

10. Quilt as desired and bind. Refer to "Finishing Your Quilt" on page 21 for more details if needed.

RESOURCES

When I want a special border for a quilt, I often refer to this book:

Kime, Janet. *The Border Workbook: Easy Speed-Pieced and Foundation-Pieced Borders* (Woodinville, Washington: Martingale & Company, 1997).

The following books have some unique and wonderful scrap quilts if you want to use the scraps left over from your fat quarter quilts:

Sloppy, Evelyn. *Strips & Strings* (Woodinville, Washington: Martingale & Company, 2003).

Speth, Pat and Thode, Charlene. *Nickel Quilts: Great Designs from 5-Inch Scraps* (Woodinville, Washington: Martingale & Company, 2002).